BY THE WOMEN OF THE LOBSTER INDUSTRY

A LOBSTER IN EVERY POT

RECIPES & LORE

EDITED BY
SUSAN K. WHITE

DESIGNED AND ILLUSTRATED BY
MAJO KELESHIAN

YANKEE BOOKS

CAMDEN · MAINE

Cover photograph © 1987 by Martha W. Nichols
Cover design by Lurelle Cheverie
Text design and illustrations by MaJo Keleshian
Imagesetting by High Resolution, Inc.
Production by Amy Fischer Design

Library of Congress Cataloging-in-Publication Data
A lobster in every pot : recipes and lore / by the Women of the Lobster Industry.
        p.   cm.
    ISBN 0-89909-216-0
    1. Cookery (Lobsters)   2. Lobsters — Folklore.   I. Women of the Lobster Industry.
TX754.L63L63   1990
641.6'95 — dc20
                                                                                    90-12669
                                                                                      CIP

A LOBSTER IN EVERY POT

RECIPES & LORE

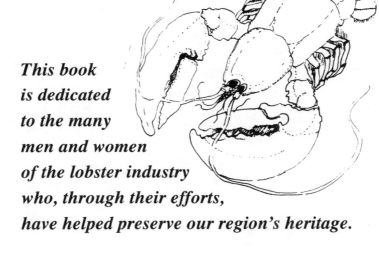

*This book
is dedicated
to the many
men and women
of the lobster industry
who, through their efforts,
have helped preserve our region's heritage.*

Contents

The **Lobster Institute** is a cooperative program of research and education between the University of Maine and the lobster industry. Established in 1987, the Institute had four founding members—the Maine Lobstermen's Association, the Maine Pound Owners Association, the Maine Import/Export Lobster Dealers Association, and the Massachusetts Lobstermen's Association. Its membership now includes companies and associations from Long Island Sound to Newfoundland and extends as far as Hawaii.

The purpose of the **Lobster Institute** is to provide information about the American lobster in order to help conserve and enhance the resource, and ensure the continuance of a strong and healthy lobster industry in Maine and the region. Royalties from this book will be used to support research and education programs of the Institute.

Preface

*T*hrough the years, the lobster industry has played a major role in the region's heritage, culture, and economy. Today, our industry and the resource it depends on are very healthy here in Maine, as well as in the rest of New England and the Maritime provinces. As we approach the twenty-first century, we have some of the largest harvests ever recorded in our 150-year history. Many credit the lobster's bright future, so rare in other fisheries of the world, to the strong conservation ethic practiced for generations by the men and women of our industry: "Take care of the resource and its environment and it, in turn, will take care of you."

The Lobster Institute is a cooperative, industry-supported research and education program at the University of Maine. Established in 1987, the Institute represents one way our industry is "taking care" to ensure the healthy future of our resource.

Our industry is grateful to the women of the lobster industry for coming up with the idea for this book; for collecting recipes, photos, and stories; and for their dedication in seeing the project through to publication by the most highly regarded cookbook publisher in New England, Yankee Books of Camden.

The Maine lobster industry takes great pride in this book, and in the women of our industry, our Lobster Institute, our University, and our lobster heritage. But there is one organization that should be recognized as the driving force behind this book and the creation of the Lobster Institute.

Without the many years of leadership of the Maine Sea Grant College Program in cooperative lobster research and advisory programs, efforts like these would not have been possible—and the future of our region's lobster industry might not be nearly so bright. All of us in the lobster industry owe a great deal to the Maine Sea Grant Program.

We hope you enjoy reading and using *A Lobster in Every Pot.* We're sure it will provide you with "the finest kind" of eating and some of the most entertaining stories and interesting facts about the "king of seafood."

Edward A. Blackmore
President and Executive Director,
Maine Lobstermen's Association
Chairman, Board of Advisors,
The Lobster Institute

Photo Credits

Illustration Credit

Acknowledgments

*T*his book would not have been possible without the efforts of many people. We would first like to thank the women on the cookbook committee who gave many hours of their time and energy to make the project a success. Members include: Jean Aldrich, Jane Alley, Mary Blackmore, Cindy Brown, Pat Carver, Myrna Coffin, Paula Colwell, Susan Hawkes, Harriet Heanssler, Roberta Joyce, Ruth Lane, Sue Nickerson, Sue Smith, and Lisa Werner.

We would also like to thank Earlon and Leta Beal, Rollins and Trenna Kelley, Pat and Richard Carver, Avery Kelley Sr., Richard Black, Ed Blackmore, Sue Smith, Connie Sullivan, Susan Hawkes, and Harriet Heanssler for contributing anecdotes for the book. In addition, Maire MacLachLan and Bethany Aronow at Northeast Archives of Folklore and Oral History at the University of Maine in Orono were very helpful in researching historical anecdotes as well as photographs.

For contributing photographs, we would like to thank Jeff Brown and the Maine State Archives in Augusta, Alicia Anstead, Robert Bayer, Richard and Roberta Black, Mary Blackmore, Pat Carver, Harriet Heanssler, Roberta Joyce, Avery Kelley Sr., Sanford Phippen, Olive Pierce, Sylvester Pollet, Bernice Skolfield, Lisa Werner, and Joanna Young.

Important contributions were also provided by Joe Vachon, former vice president of the Maine Lobstermen's Association; Robin Tara, a premier lobster lover; Robert Bayer, University of Maine lobster biologist; Sue Russell, secretary for the Sea Grant Marine Advisory Program; Joyce Wheeler, University of Maine System; David Dow, Executive Director of the Lobster Institute; and Jean Day, also of the Lobster Institute. Thanks, also, to Acadia Publishing Company of Bar Harbor and Mount Desert Oceanarium in Southwest Harbor. Finally, we would like to thank the University's Center for Marine Studies for their support.

Cook's Introduction

When I was growing up, and for years after I left home, I was convinced there was only one thing to do with lobster—boil them and eat them. No great mystery, no measuring, no timing, no frills—nothing but pools of butter for dipping.

My father loves to eat. He is motivated by food. He always made it his business to know where the fiddleheads grew, where the trout were biting, and where to pick wild strawberries. He cultivated friendships with farmers who allowed him to pick his own sweet corn and fresh peas. And, best of all, he knew lobstermen. He would make the hour's drive to Blue Hill just to see his friend Seth and come home with a dozen lobsters for supper. He would duck through the kitchen (he is a tall man!) carrying a huge ice chest in his arms. He'd take off the cover, lift out a lively, thrashing lobster, and say, "Look at the claws on that one!" He liked them big and he liked them hard-shelled. He ate only the claws—my mother ate the tails and picked the bodies. While the salted water came to a boil in the big pot we used only for lobster, clams, and corn on the cob, my brothers and I would hold lobster races on the kitchen linoleum. When the time was right, my father would plunge the lobsters head first into the boiling water. By the time the water reached a boil again, my mother would put on the butter to melt. When it was done, we'd be ready for our feast.

In my family, when we ate lobsters, we did just that—we ate lobsters. No salad, no vegetables—just some saltines for mother to put tomalley on. It was the same routine with steamed clams and corn on the cob. We didn't just eat them plain—we ate them *alone*.

Although I ate a lot of lobster as a child, I could never get enough of them. I guess it's no wonder I married a lobsterman. For the first few months of marriage, I reveled in boiled lobsters. It seemed there was an endless supply. As time went on, I started to experiment—first with the stews, pies, and salads, and then on to the more exotic canapés, quiches, and soufflés. I was lucky to have among my friends other lobstermen's wives who shared with me their family recipes.

I believe the world is made up of two kinds of people—those who love lobster and those who don't. This cookbook was written to please the former. In its pages, you'll find hundreds of ways to cook lobster. For the host or hostess, there are elegant lobster appetizers—a sure way to impress your guests. The gourmet can indulge in lobster curry, crêpes or creole. And, even if you're like Ruth Lane and "like it plain," you'll discover that there really is more than one way to cook a lobster.

A Lobster Lover

*t*he American lobster, *Homarus americanus,* is synonymous with the Maine coast. Even when it is trapped in other places on the east coast of North America, it is often referred to as "Maine lobster."

Lobsters have been fished commercially in Maine since the mid-1800s. In the past thirty years, the lobster has become a gourmet seafood item. Its sweet, tender meat has excited the palate of connoisseurs throughout the world. And, there is just nothing like the beautiful, bright red color of a freshly-cooked lobster.

Many people, however, are intimidated by lobsters. This book will explain how to buy, cook, and eat lobsters, and provide some delicious "tried-and-true" recipes for many ways to serve them.

Chapter 1
BASICS:
How to Start

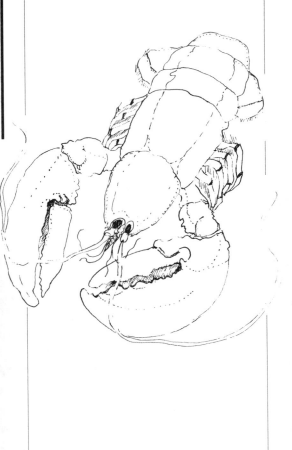

Gouldsboro, 1946

Fig. 1

When you buy a lobster, how do you tell if it's alive?

Only buy a live lobster. As long as the lobster is moving—either its legs, antennae, or flipping its tail—it is alive. Lobsters should always be alive before cooking. A cooked lobster should have a tail that is curled, indicating that it was alive when cooked.

How many lobsters do I need to buy?

If lobster is to be served whole, a 1- to 2-pound lobster serves one person.

How many live lobsters make a pound of meat?

It is difficult to say exactly how many live lobsters it takes to make a pound of meat, mainly because lobsters contain more meat at different times of the year. According to Donald Look of A. M. Look Canning Company of East Machias, in the middle of the winter when lobsters are most full of meat, it takes about $4\frac{1}{2}$ pounds of live lobsters to get a pound of meat. However, in the late summer, when lobsters have shed, it takes about nine 1-pound live lobsters to get a pound of meat.

On average, it takes about **six 1-pound live lobsters to equal a pound of meat.**

How many cups of lobster meat are in one pound?

Approximately two cups of meat equal one pound.

How do you hold a lobster so you aren't pinched?

Hold it at the end of the carapace where it joins the tail (Figure 1). Many cooks prefer to leave the bands on the claws when they cook lobsters to avoid being pinched. (Bands also prevent lobsters from damaging themselves.)

If you cook lobsters with rubber bands on the claws, does it make them taste like rubber?

Tests conducted at the University of Maine showed there was no taste difference between lobsters cooked with rubber bands on the claws and those cooked with no bands.

How do you pack live lobsters to travel?

Put lobsters in a styrofoam or insulated outer box packed with ice. To prevent lobsters from coming into contact with fresh water, ice should be enclosed in plastic bags. Cover lobsters with seaweed if possible. Lobsters packed in ice will last at least a day.

How long can you keep live lobsters in a refrigerator? How long will they stay alive?

Live lobsters can be kept for approximately 12 hours under refrigerated conditions although most will survive for at least 24 hours. Keep them covered with a damp cloth or a layer of seaweed to provide moisture. Live lobsters **cannot** be stored in fresh water or enclosed in plastic bags.

How long can you keep cooked lobster in the refrigerator?

It will probably be good for 3 to 4 days.

When is lobster less expensive to buy? Why?

In Maine, lobsters are less expensive from the end of August to the beginning of November because this is when most lobsters are harvested.

What's the difference between a hard-shell and soft-shell lobster? Is one a better bargain?

When a lobster outgrows its shell, it molts and discards or "sheds" the old shell. It then has a soft shell and is called a "shedder." As the lobster feeds, its shell hardens, and it adds meat to its body. Soft-shell lobsters have less meat than hard-shell lobsters, but their shells also weigh less. Since you buy lobsters according to their weight, they are about the same in terms of price. It should be noted, however, that hard-shell lobsters usually survive longer in the refrigerator than ones that have soft shells.

"...not in fresh water"
Some years back a young doctor came to town to start his practice. A fisherman welcomed him with a number of fresh lobsters. The new doctor knew nothing about lobsters so, wanting to keep them alive, he put them in the bathtub in fresh water. He was pretty upset to come back and find his lobsters dead.

Harriet Heanssler, Deer Isle (1989)

Richard Black, Bass Harbor, 1960

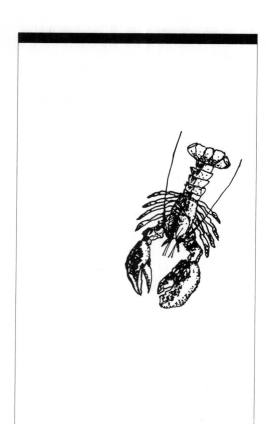

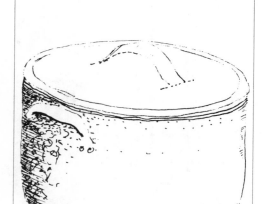

Is it okay to eat a soft-shell lobster?

Yes. Some people prefer soft-shell lobsters because they say the meat is a little sweeter and they don't need any tools to crack them apart.

How often does a lobster molt?

Lobsters molt about twenty-five times in the first 5 to 7 years of their lives. After that time, they molt less frequently—about once a year. After a molt, it takes months for a shell to harden and fill with meat.

How much do lobsters gain in size when they shed?

They increase about 20 percent each time.

How much water is necessary to boil a lobster? Should you use salt water?

Put one to two inches of water in the bottom of the pot to steam lobsters, or allow $2\frac{1}{2}$ quarts of water per lobster if you want to boil them. You don't have to use saltwater, but some people believe lobsters taste better if you add salt to the water or use seawater, which contains $2\frac{1}{2}$ to 3 percent salt. (For complete instructions on how to cook lobsters, read further in this chapter.)

How do you tell when a lobster is done?

If the antennae pull out easily, the lobster is done.

Why do lobsters turn red when they are cooked?

A live lobster is greenish-brown because of many different color pigment *chromatophores*. When it is cooked, all the pigments are masked except for *astaxanthin,* which is the background red pigment.

Does lobster contain much fat or cholesterol?

Lobster (without butter) is very low in calories, saturated fat, and cholesterol. It has less fat than flounder, and about the same amount of cholesterol. Lobster meat also contains omega-3 unsaturated fatty acids, the substances that seem to reduce hardening of the arteries and decrease the risk of heart disease. (Figure 2)

Lobster is good and *good for you!*

3.5 ounces	Calories	Grams of Saturated Fat	Grams of Protein	Milligrams of Cholesterol
Clams	74	0.3	15.6	25
Cod	75	0.1	22.8	45
Lobster	90	0.1	20	80
Milk (8 oz.)	150	5.0	8	33
Eggs (2)	158	3.4	11.2	550
Chicken (lt.meat)	163	1.3	30.9	85
Ground Beef (lean)	268	7.0	28	100
Sirloin Steak (broiled)	280	7.5	30	95

PLUS... Lobster meat contains omega-3 fatty acids, the substances that seem to reduce hardening of the arteries and decrease the risk of heart disease.

Lobsters do **not** accumulate the Paralytic Shellfish Poisoning (PSP) toxin from the natural phenomenon, "red tide," which sometimes occurs along the coast in the summer.

Lobster is also high in:

• amino acids, which are the building blocks of proteins and very important for growth. The amino acid lysine is believed to help prevent Herpes outbreaks.
• potassium and magnesium, which help the body make proteins, promote muscular strength (including the heart), and transmit nerve impulses.
• vitamins B12, B6, B3 (niacin), and B2 (riboflavin), which produce energy, support healthy skin, and are good for the nervous system.
• calcium and phosphorous for healthy bones and teeth.
• iron, which makes a strong body and helps it resist infection.
• zinc, which is important for growth, healing wounds, and sexual development.
• vitamin A, which promotes good vision as well as growth of bones and teeth.

Fig. 2

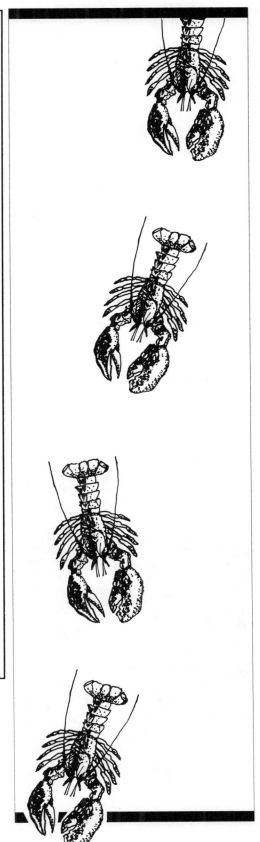

What part of the lobster is tomalley?

The tomalley functions like a combination intestine, liver, and pancreas in the lobster. Some people think this is the best part of the lobster to eat.

Is it necessary to remove the black vein in the tail before eating?

It won't hurt you, but some people prefer to remove it because it is the intestine which is part of the digestive system and does not taste very good.

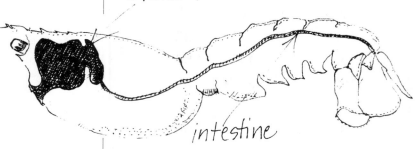

What is the sac? Why remove it?

The sac is the stomach of the lobster and is located behind the eyes. Many recipes say that the sac should be removed because it can be filled with shell particles, bones from bait, and digestive juices that are not very tasty.

What is the red part that you sometimes see inside a lobster?

These are the roe or unfertilized eggs which have not been extruded. It is called "coral" and some people find it very tasty.

Are there parts of a lobster that are poisonous?

No.

What are "culls"?

Lobsters that have lost one or both claws. It takes three or four molts for a lobster to regenerate a claw to full size.

Why does a lobster drop a claw?

A lobster can drop a claw as a defense mechanism and grow another over a period of years.

What are chickens, quarters, selects, and jumbos?

The following common terms are used to describe the size of

The Lobster Pound Restaurant, Lincolnville

lobsters, according to the Maine Department of Marine Resources:

1-pound: *chickens*
1-pound to $1^{1}/_{8}$-pound: *heavy chickens*
$1^{1}/_{4}$-pound: *quarters*
$1^{1}/_{2}$- to $1^{3}/_{4}$-pound: *selects*
2-pound: *deuces* or *2-pounders*
2- to $2^{1}/_{4}$-pound: *heavy selects*
$2^{1}/_{4}$- to $2^{1}/_{2}$-pound: *small jumbos*
Over $2^{1}/_{2}$-pound to approximately 4-pound: *jumbos*

What are "shorts" or "snappers"?

They are undersized lobsters that a lobsterman throws back into the ocean so they can grow to legal size.

What are "canner" lobsters?

Canners are smaller lobsters caught only in the Gulf of St. Lawrence in Canada. At one time, all of these lobsters went into a cannery. Since the water is warmer in this area, lobsters mature at a smaller size. It is legal to catch small lobsters only in this region.

Are large lobsters tougher than small lobsters?

Most people think there is no difference in tenderness between the meat of small and large lobsters. However, cooking a lobster for too long can make it tough. Also, according to some people, meat from soft-shell lobsters is more tender than that from hard-shell lobsters.

How old is an old lobster?

No one has yet found a way to determine the exact age of a lobster because it sheds its shell every time it molts.

Is the "Maine lobster," Homarus americanus, found only in Maine?

No, it's found on the east coast from Newfoundland to North Carolina. There are many other kinds of lobsters found in other parts of the world.

Is a crayfish a baby lobster?

No. Crayfish are related to lobsters but they live in fresh or brackish water. Lobsters live only in saltwater.

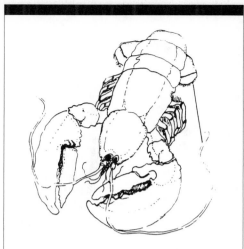

Lobsters Hanging from the Trees!
My mother-in-law told me one time there was a hurricane down on the back side of the island. The day after the hurricane she walked down there and there were lobsters hanging in the trees. The wind blew so hard and there was so much surf, it washed the lobsters right up into the tops of the fir trees.

Pat Carver, Beals (1990)

Lobster Cooked the Plain Way

Ruth Lane, Secretary/Treasurer of the Maine Lobstermen's Association, wrote the following letter when she was asked to contribute some recipes for our cookbook:

"Enclosed are some recipes I found. I don't eat enough lobster that I'm ever tired of them plain boiled. I tried a few of the recipes but I found I had a hard time being objective. I like lobster plain.

I asked a few of my friends but they eat lobster plain, too. I made some of the casseroles and fed it to the kids. 'Too bad to cover up the taste of lobster,' they said. Oh well, what can I say? We like it plain."

How to Cook Lobsters

The two most common ways to cook lobsters are steaming and boiling. Most fishermen prefer to steam lobsters.

To **steam** lobsters, put about 2 inches of seawater or salted fresh water in the bottom of a large kettle. Bring the water to a rolling boil. Put in the live lobsters, one at a time, grasping just behind the claws. Let the water boil again and begin timing. Allow 18 minutes for a 1- to 1^1/$_4$-pound hard-shell lobster and 20 minutes for a 1^1/$_2$-pound hard-shell lobster. If the lobster has a soft shell, reduce the cooking time by 3 minutes.

To **boil** lobsters, fill a large kettle three-quarters full of water. If seawater is not available, add 2 tablespoons of salt for each quart of water. A good rule of thumb is to allow 2^1/$_2$ quarts of water for each lobster. Bring the water to a boil. Put in the live lobsters one at a time and let the water boil again. Lower the heat, cover the kettle, and simmer about 15 minutes for 1-to 1^1/$_4$-pound hard-shell lobsters and 20 minutes for 1^1/$_2$- to 2-pound hard-shell lobsters. Again, soft-shell lobsters take a little less time, so reduce the cooking time by 3 minutes. When the antennae pull out easily, the lobsters are done. Serve whole lobster, either hot or cold, with a side dish of melted butter.

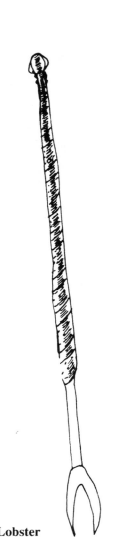

How to Cook a Lobster without a Pot!

Lester and I fished winters together. When we went offshore and we wanted a lobster to eat, we'd save 2 or 3 lobsters and I'd go on top of the windshield over the exhaust pipe and hold a 10-quart pail with a little bit of salt water in it and boil my lobsters in it. We'd be going 4 or 5 miles to our offshore string and by the time we got there, those lobsters were all boiled. Lester'd say, "Rockefeller can't have lobsters this way!"

Earlon Beal, Beals (1990)

Department of Sea and Shore Fisheries promotion (now Maine Department of Marine Resources), 1959

How to Eat Lobsters

1. Twist off the large claws.

2. Crack each claw with a nutcracker, pliers, knife, hammer, or rock.

3. Separate the tail from the body by arching the back until it cracks.

4. Break off the tail flippers.

5. Insert a fork (or a thumb) and push the tail meat out in one piece. Remove and discard the black vein which runs the entire length of the tail.

6. Unhinge the back shell from the body. The green part in the body cavity is the tomalley, which many people consider the most delicious part of the lobster. The coral-colored roe is also edible.

7. Open the body by cracking it apart sideways. Lobster meat lies in the four pockets (or joints) where the small walking legs are attached. The small walking legs also contain excellent meat which can be removed by sucking.

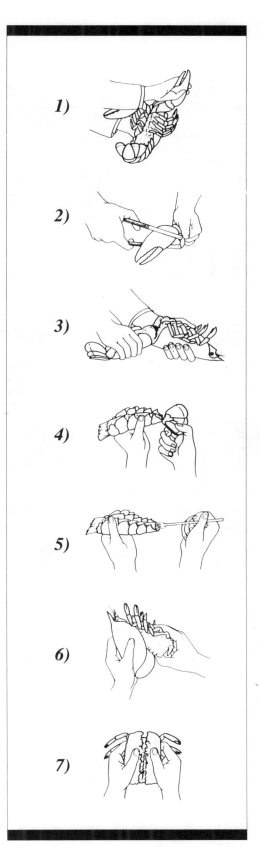

1)
2)
3)
4)
5)
6)
7)

How to Split a Live Lobster for Broiling and Baking

1. Place the lobster on its back. Cross the large claws over its head and hold firmly with your left hand. Make a deep, quick incision with a sharp, pointed knife and draw the knife quickly down the entire length of the body and tail.

2. Spread the lobster flat. Remove the tomalley and roe. Break the intestinal vein where it is attached to the end of the tail. With your fingers remove the sac or stomach. This will break the other end of the intestinal tract. Remove the intestine. Clean the cavity by holding under cold running water, if necessary. Drain well.

Mary Blackmore, Stonington

How to Microwave a Whole Lobster

1. Plunge the tip of a heavy knife into a live lobster between its head and first segment. Lobster may show signs of movement for a few minutes.

2. Peg the tail to prevent curling by inserting a wooden skewer lengthwise through the meat. At this time, or after the lobster is cooked, cut through the under shell of the body and remove the intestinal vein and small sac below the head.

3. Arrange lobster in a 9x12-inch baking dish with the back down and add $1/2$ cup hot water. Cover tightly with plastic wrap turning back a corner to vent. Microwave on high, turning over after 6 minutes. Total cooking time is 9 to 12 minutes.

Pat Carver, Beals

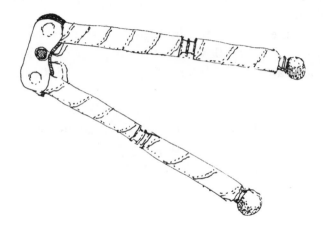

Lobster Tails on the Gas Grill

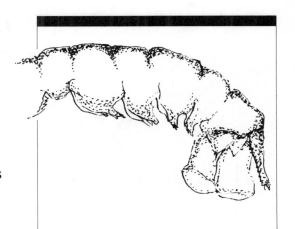

1. Snap tails off live lobsters. Remove and discard the under shell on the tail section. Insert skewer lengthwise through the tail at both ends to prevent curling as it cooks or clamp tightly in a double wire broiler.

2. Place lobsters shell side down on grill grates set in high position. Grill for 5 minutes on medium heat. Turn tails during cooking, grilling the other side for 6 to 7 minutes. Return tails to shell side down position and baste meat with melted butter mixed with lemon juice.

To snap off tails:
This is best accomplished by using a small pair of culinary shears. Holding the tail with the hard outer shell down in the palm of your hand, snip around the outside edge of the thinner under shell to expose the tail meat.

To insert the skewer:
Make sure the skewer pierces the hard shell at both ends. Put as many tails as will fit on a skewer. Repeat.

Gregory Griffin, Cape Elizabeth

Fried Lobster

Melt butter in a skillet and put in cooked lobster meat. Fry until meat is a bit browned. Add vinegar to taste.

Louise Alley, South Bristol

from *Deep Waters* magazine

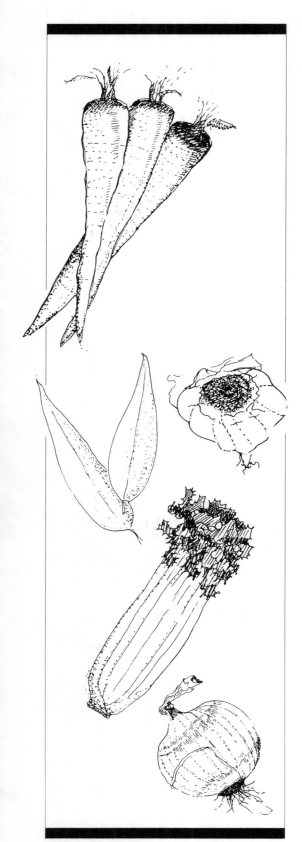

Lobster Stock

head, shells, and legs of 2 or more lobsters
2 quarts water (including water in which lobsters were cooked)
$^1/_2$ cup onion, chopped or sliced
$^1/_2$ cup celery, chopped, plus a handful of celery leaves
$^1/_2$ cup carrots, chopped
1 clove garlic, halved
2 or 3 sprigs of fresh parsley (or 1 teaspoon parsley flakes)
$^1/_2$ teaspoon salt
1 small bay leaf
5 or 6 whole peppercorns
2 or 3 whole cloves or allspice
$^1/_4$ teaspoon thyme or sage

     1. Bring all ingredients to a rolling boil, lower the heat, and simmer gently for 30 to 40 minutes. Cool, strain, and refrigerate.
     2. Pour into 1-pint (or 8-ounce) containers, leaving expansion space. Label and freeze. This stock may be used as a court bouillon for cooking shrimp, in sauces for fish, or for bisques.

Linda Kelsey, South Bristol

Preparing Lobsters for Storage or Freezing

     1. After lobsters have cooked the proper time (see How to Cook Lobsters on page 8), remove from cooker and rinse with cold water until cool enough to handle. Remove from shell, following directions of How to Eat Lobsters. Remove tail first, pull back tail flap, and remove vein. Throw away any lobster tail meat that doesn't come out whole or that crumbles into small sections.
     2. Place all meat into a saltwater bath made by mixing $^1/_4$ cup salt with 1 gallon water. Stir gently, then rinse in colander, and package. It may be stored in the refrigerator or frozen.

Bob Brown, Lusty Lobster, Portland

Substitutions

*T*he recipes in this book were contributed by the women of the lobster industry. Many of them were handed down from their mothers or grandmothers and call for whole, natural ingredients. With the increasing emphasis on diets that are low in saturated fat and cholesterol, we decided to include some substitutions that contain fewer calories and less fat, but still make the dishes taste delicious.

Butter: Margarine has less saturated fat and cholesterol than butter. Two teaspoons of vegetable oil may be used in place of 1 tablespoon of butter or margarine. Oil also has fewer calories.

Cream: Evaporated milk, either whole or skim, may be substituted.

Milk: To make 1 cup of whole milk, mix 1/2 cup of evaporated whole milk with 1/2 cup of water. Another substitution is to mix 4 tablespoons of powdered milk with 1 cup of water.

Sour Cream: Yogurt may be used in place of sour cream in most recipes, although it gives a slightly tangier taste to the dish. Also, you can purée 1 cup of cottage or part-skim ricotta cheese in a blender for a low-fat version, or combine the cheese with 2 tablespoons of skim milk and 1 tablespoon of lemon juice. Another suggestion is to whip 1/2 cup of chilled evaporated milk with 1 tablespoon of white vinegar and use it in place of 1 cup of sour cream.

Cream Cheese: Blend 1 cup of low-fat cottage cheese with 1/4 cup margarine to equal 1 cup cream cheese. This is lower in saturated fat and cholesterol but not lower in total fat.

Bread Crumbs: Replace 1 cup of bread crumbs with 3/4 cup of cracker or cereal crumbs.

Sweeteners: For most dessert recipes, the amount of sweetener may be reduced by one-third or one-half. To substitute honey for sugar, reduce the amount by 25 percent. (3/4 cup honey equals 1 cup sugar.) To make 1 cup of brown sugar, combine 1 cup of white sugar with 1/4 cup of molasses.

Port Clyde, 1940

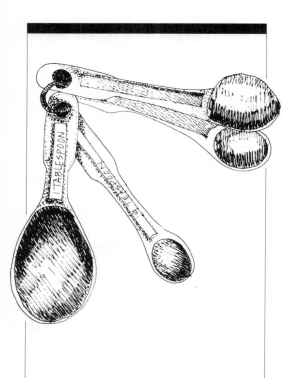

Wholesome Ways to Thicken Soups and Sauces

Soups: There are several ways to thicken creamed soups using skim milk instead of heavy cream. One is to add grated raw potato to the broth and cook for 5 minutes before adding the milk. Another is to use cornstarch instead of flour as the thickening agent. By using cornstarch, butter is not needed. Mix 1 tablespoon of cornstarch with 2 tablespoons of cold water, and stir the mixture until it is smooth. Add 2 tablespoons of the hot liquid, stir, and then add the whole mixture to the liquid you wish to thicken.

Sauces: Puréed low-fat cottage cheese or part-skim ricotta may be used as the base or as part of the liquid ingredients. A tablespoon of mashed potatoes may also be whisked into the sauce.

Gouldsboro, 1946

$m$outh-watering appetizers stimulate the appetite before a meal. The recipes offered here will do just that. Whether you serve them to your family, anxiously awaiting the main course, or to your guests at the start of a summer seafood fest, they are sure to delight.

For the information you will need to cook lobster and remove the meat from its shell, please refer to "Chapter 1, Basics: How to Start." All the following recipes can be made with leftover lobster. They can be a meal in themselves or a delicious accompaniment to a hearty, homemade soup and a crisp, green salad. Bon appetit!

Chapter 2

BEFORE THE FEAST:

Appetizers

Bass Harbor, 1987

Appetizers   15

Lobster Cocktail

For each cocktail, allow:
> 1/4 cup lobster meat, cut in pieces
> 2 tablespoons tomato catsup
> 2 tablespoons sherry
> 1 tablespoon lemon juice
> 4 drops Worcestershire sauce
> salt to taste
> chives, chopped

Mix well and chill. Serve in cocktail glasses, sprinkled with chopped chives.

Pat Poitras, Stonington

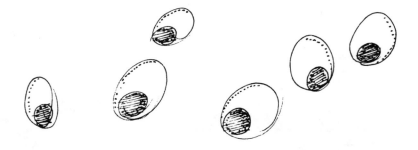

Lobster Dip with Cream Cheese and Olives

8 ounces cream cheese
1 cup cooked lobster meat, ground in blender or meat grinder
1 small bottle green olives, finely chopped
1 tablespoon onion, chopped
1 tablespoon mayonnaise
1 teaspoon lemon juice

Combine all ingredients. Chill overnight in the refrigerator for best results. Shrimp or crabmeat may be combined with the lobster. This dip is good on bagels, crackers, or toasted bread rounds.

Rose Gove, Stonington

Spicy Lobster Dip

$^1/_2$ cup mayonnaise
$1^1/_4$ cups cooked lobster meat, chopped
$^3/_4$ cup celery, diced
$^1/_2$ teaspoon salt
1 teaspoon lemon juice
$^1/_2$ teaspoon onion salt
$^1/_4$ teaspoon curry powder
$^1/_2$ teaspoon Worcestershire sauce

Combine all ingredients and refrigerate for at least four hours before serving. Serve with cut fresh vegetables.

Harriet Bisset, Ellsworth

A Riddle

I have three ribs and no backbone
Two heads with a mouth in each.
I spend part of my life in the seaweed and kelp
And part on the sandy beach.
I begin my life on the hard, dry land
But soon in the water I go
For a long embrace in the arms of the deep
And a home where the tides ebb and flow.

Answer: Lobster Trap

Mrs. E. R. Peasley, Jonesport (1961)
Northeast Archives #15225

Traps Have Many Uses
A fellow had his traps on the boat all ready to set. When he boarded the boat and untied her, he noticed a duck sitting on a trap. Figuring the duck would fly off, he proceeded. The duck stayed aboard as the traps were set out. All of a sudden the duck began quacking and flapping her wings in desperation. The fellow hauled back the trap he had just set and found one egg inside. He removed the egg and set it aside but it was too late. The mother duck circled the boat and flew toward shore.

Susan Smith, Kittery Point (1989)

What is the difference between lobster "pots" and lobster "traps"?
They are the same thing. The terminology varies from one part of the coast to another.

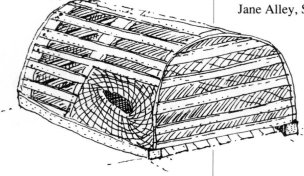

Lobster Spread

1 cup cooked lobster meat, finely chopped
1 tablespoon onion, finely chopped
1 tablespoon green pepper, finely chopped
4 to 6 tablespoons mayonnaise

Combine lobster meat, onion, and green pepper in a bowl. Mix with mayonnaise to spreading consistency. Serve on crackers or as a filling for finger sandwiches.

Jane Alley, South Bristol

Lobster Paste

2^1/$_2$ cups cooked lobster meat, finely chopped
^{1}/$_2$ cup apple cider vinegar
1 egg unbeaten
1 tablespoon flour
1 tablespoon prepared mustard
1^1/$_2$ tablespoons sugar
^{3}/$_4$ teaspoon salt
1 tablespoon butter, melted and cooled

1. Heat the vinegar in a double boiler.
2. Mix the dry ingredients in a mixing bowl. Add the unbeaten egg and melted butter, and blend well.
3. Pour the hot vinegar slowly over the mixture.
4. Place the sauce in double boiler. Cook until well thickened. Cool.
5. Add the chopped lobster meat and mix well. Serve on crackers, melba toast, or slices of French bread.
Makes 1 cup.

Paula Colwell, Deer Isle

Lobster Eggs

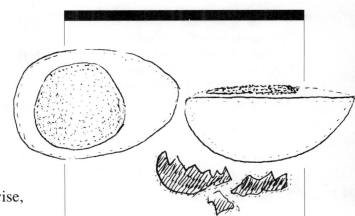

6 eggs, hard-boiled
$^{1}/_{2}$ cup cooked lobster meat, chopped
$2^{1}/_{2}$ tablespoons tartar sauce (see recipe below)
12 pieces of bread (cut in oval shapes), sautéed in butter
mayonnaise
watercress

   1. Prepare hard-boiled eggs; cut in halves lengthwise, and remove yolks.
   2. Fill the whites with chopped lobster meat moistened with tartar sauce and invert on sautéed bread.
   3. Pipe yolk that has been mixed with a little mayonnaise over the egg and garnish with a tip of the watercress.

Paula Colwell, Deer Isle

Tartar Sauce
$^{3}/_{4}$ cup mayonnaise
$^{1}/_{4}$ tablespoon onion, finely chopped
$^{1}/_{2}$ tablespoon capers (optional)
$^{1}/_{2}$ tablespoon sweet pickles, finely chopped
$^{1}/_{2}$ tablespoon olives, finely chopped
$^{1}/_{2}$ tablespoon fresh parsley, finely chopped
1 tablespoon tarragon (or red wine) vinegar
Combine all ingredients and keep refrigerated.

Hills of Mt. Desert Island, 1988

How are lobsters caught?
The lobster walks up the head of the trap which is made of net, looking for the bait that is inside. It enters the "kitchen" or forward compartment of the trap, and usually tries to escape—and sometimes succeeds. When it tries to escape, it may find its way into the "parlor." Lobsters rarely escape from this part of the trap.

Hauling traps at Pemaquid

*H*ere are some simple but delicious ways to use leftover lobster in appetizers. In those recipes that do not list specific quantities, use your best judgment.

Lobster Canapés I

Finely chop any amount of cooked lobster meat and season with salt, pepper, lemon juice, olive oil, and Tabasco sauce. Lobster should be moist enough to spread easily on toasted cuts of bread. Garnish with paprika.

Paula Colwell, Deer Isle

Lobster Canapés II

Cut slices of bread in 2-inch rounds and sauté in olive oil. Blend finely chopped, well-seasoned, cooked lobster meat with creamed butter and Worcestershire sauce. Make mounds of this mixture on the sautéed bread. Top with olive slices and paprika.

Paula Colwell, Deer Isle

Lobster Canapés III

Preheat oven to 350°. Chop leftover lobster meat into small pieces. Cut crusts from bread. Arrange lobster meat on bread slices, roll up, and stick with toothpicks. Arrange in baking pan. Butter tops. Bake until toasted. Cut each "roll-up" in half and serve.

Mabel Haskell, Stonington

Curried Hot Lobster Canapés

2 tablespoons butter
2 teaspoons onion, chopped
2 tablespoons watercress leaves, chopped
2 teaspoons flour
1 teaspoon curry powder
$^1/_2$ cup cooked lobster meat, finely chopped
bread slices
pimento strips, for garnish

    1. Melt butter in an omelette pan. Add chopped onion and watercress, and let cook until soft but not brown.
    2. Add flour mixed with curry powder. When well blended, add lobster meat.
    3. Cut bread in pieces $1^1/_4$ inches wide and $2^1/_2$ inches long. Sauté in olive oil. Spread crusts with hot lobster mixture and place tiny strips of pimento diagonally across the tops.

Paula Colwell, Deer Isle

Spruce Head, 1989

Early Morning Reflections
Sometimes before it's daylight and you're just right off and there're no islands between you and the horizon, you can see the sun come out of the water and there's nothing like it! If you think sunsets are pretty, you should see a sunrise—you know one of those good, clear, calm days that the water is just like a sheet of glass you might say and it's just reflections. Makes you get up in the morning just to see it.

Ken Horr, Long Island (1973)
Northeast Archives #750088

Tomalley Appetizer

tomalley from 1 cooked lobster
mayonnaise
paprika
scallion
crackers

Mix tomalley with a small amount of mayonnaise. Place on crackers, sprinkle with paprika, and top with a thin slice of scallion.

Gretchen Stearns, Stonington

A Sea of Many Colors
You talk about different-colored buoys. I don't know as you could name any color that you wouldn't find among lobster fishermen painted on our buoys. And when it's a calm, beautiful day, sometimes as far as you can see, there's a display of all these different-colored buoys and it's a beautiful scene. When the water is perfectly calm and just like a mirror, it's a beautiful scene because you'd see all these different-colored buoys.

Henry Walls, Vinalhaven (1973)
Northeast Archives #7710009

Gardner Gross, Stonington, 1984

South Harpswell, 1947

Lobster Croquettes

2 cups cooked lobster meat, finely chopped
1 stick butter
$^1/_4$ cup onion, finely chopped
$^1/_4$ cup celery, finely chopped
$^1/_8$ cup green pepper, finely chopped
1 cup cream
$^1/_4$ cup bread crumbs
salt and pepper
2 eggs, beaten
bread crumbs for coating

     1. Sauté onions, celery, and green pepper in butter until tender.
     2. Add lobster meat and remove from heat.
     3. Add cream, bread crumbs, salt, and pepper to taste.
     4. Chill, and shape into croquettes.
     5. Dip into well-beaten eggs and roll in bread crumbs.
Fry in deep fat at 375° for 3 to 4 minutes.

Ruth Prior, Bremen

Why do some fishermen use wood and others use wire traps?
Wooden traps are the traditional style used by lobstermen for over one hundred years. Wire traps are more common to-day because they are much lighter, easier to handle, and they last longer.

Hills of Mt. Desert Island, 1988

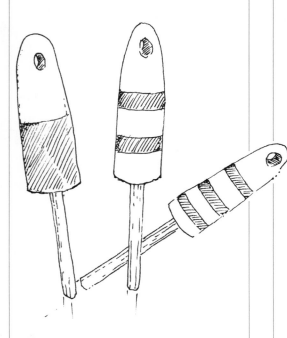

Why do lobster buoys have different colors and numbers on them?
Fishermen use different designs and colors so they can identify their traps.

Breakfast for a Gull

I was rowing along one beautiful, calm morning in the month of August along Green Island's shore. As a rule, I always put my lobsters in front of myself after I've caught them, so I could be aware of the gulls and they wouldn't steal my lobsters. As it happened this morning, I put my lobster tub behind me and this gull was very wise. He knew that I was back to and he flew down and took a lobster out of my tub—and he weighed just about two pounds. What a peculiar sight! He stole that lobster and there he was going through the air. He knew how to grip that lobster not to get bit.

And there he was going to shore. He went ashore right on Green's Island and I stopped and watched him. He laid down the lobster and he drove his bill down into that lobster and he broke him apart and began eating it.

Henry Walls, Vinalhaven (1973)
Northeast Archives #7710016

*N*othing hits the spot on a cold, wintery Maine day like a steaming bowl of chowder. And rich, creamy lobster chowders, bisques, and stews are the perfect foods to brighten up the day.

In this chapter, you will also find lobster quiches, puffs, stuffing for peppers, and other simple entrées which take a minimum of preparation and cooking time, yet taste like you've spent hours in the kitchen.

Chapter 3

A LIGHT COURSE:

Soups, Quiches, and Other Simple Entrées

Amanda and Tamya, 1987

Cindy's Lobster Bisque with Egg

1¹/₂-pound live lobster
1 stick butter
3 tablespoons flour
3¹/₂ cups milk
¹/₂ teaspoon salt
¹/₄ teaspoon pepper
¹/₄ teaspoon celery salt
1 egg, separated

1. Steam the lobster. Remove meat and chop into small pieces.

2. Melt butter in deep saucepan over low flame. Add flour, blend until very smooth, and gradually add milk, stirring constantly until thickened.

3. Add salt, pepper, and celery salt and simmer 5 minutes.

4. Beat egg yolk in a deep bowl until foamy and then add lobster meat.

5. Add the lobster and egg to the milk mixture in the saucepan. Heat thoroughly, but *do not allow to boil*.

6. Beat egg white until stiff and place it in a warmed (not hot) soup tureen. Pour the lobster bisque over the beaten egg white, stirring carefully. Serve immediately.

Cindy Brown, North Edgecomb

Maine Seafoods Festival, Rockland, 1965

How does a lobster "smell" its food?
The lobster "smells" or senses its food by using four small antennae located on the front of its head and by tiny sensing hairs that cover its body.

Harry's Lobster Bisque

1 cup cooked lobster meat, finely chopped
1 1/2 sticks butter (unsalted)
1/2 cup flour
1/2 teaspoon thyme, fresh if available
salt and pepper to taste
1/2 handful parsley flakes or chopped fresh parsley, if available
6 tablespoons golden sherry
4 cups cream (half and half)

   1. Sauté lobster in butter. Add flour, thyme, salt and pepper, and parsley. Cook for 5 minutes over low heat.
   2. Add sherry and half and half. Cook for 1 hour, stirring every 5 minutes. Serve with crackers or croutons. This is better if cooked the day before and reheated.

Serves 6.

Harry Moulin, Ellsworth

"Grampy's" Lobster Chowder

1 large onion, diced
3 tablespoons butter
4 large potatoes, diced
1/2 cup water
2 to 3 cups cooked lobster meat
4 cups whole milk
salt and pepper to taste

   1. Sauté onion in butter until soft.
   2. Add potato with about 1/2 cup water. Then boil gently until tender or about 10 minutes.
   3. Add lobster pieces and milk and heat thoroughly, but *do not boil*. Use part cream, if desired.

Serve with hot rolls and green salad.

Donna Vachon, Stetson

"... just like my dad"
Devin was a true lobsterman's son. He was barely two months old his first Christmas when he got his first boat—a three-foot-long Gloucester dory with rockers on the bottom painted the same clear sky blue as his dad's boat. Quite a bit of playpen time was spent that first early spring in the shop watching dad cut ropes and mend traps. So, it seemed logical that a toggle and buoy were among his favorite toys—and soon were among his first words.

Now, regardless of weather or season, Devin spent a part of every day clomping around in red rubber boots, his "dory" piled high with plastic sweater boxes and open plastic storage crates. When asked what he was doing, he'd tell you "Settin' my gear" or "Goin' to get bait." The sweater boxes were very carefully arranged around the house, and heaven help the person who dared to touch his "traps!" The crates were raised and lowered from the kitchen table or the picnic table to "get bait" and returned to the dory.

Finally, Devin returned to the mooring, driving an old trap with a steering wheel nailed to it—a wheel that his great-grandfather made when dad was a toddler. If you ever asked this three-year-old what he wanted to be when he grew up, the answer was quick and simple—"A lobsterman just like my dad."

Connie Sullivan, Kittery (1989)

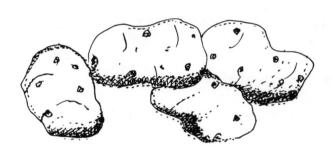

Fish and Lobster Chowder

1¹/₂ pounds halibut
1¹/₂ cups water
1¹/₂ pound lobster
4 tablespoons butter or margarine
1 large onion, sliced
2 slices salt pork or 4 tablespoons butter
4 cups raw potatoes, cubed
2 teaspoons salt
¹/₈ teaspoon pepper
4 cups milk

1. Simmer the halibut in water for about 15 minutes or until it flakes easily when tested with a fork. Reserve the cooking liquid.

2. Cook lobster, cool, and remove meat. Cut lobster meat in generous pieces and sauté it slowly in butter to bring out rosy color.

3. Fry the salt pork (or melt butter), add onion slices and cook until golden.

4. In a stew kettle, combine salt pork scraps (if used) with onion and potatoes. Add water to barely cover the ingredients, and cook until the potatoes are tender. Then add cooking liquid from the fish.

5. Remove skin and bones from the fish and break into bite-sized pieces. Add fish, lobster, milk, and seasonings. Taste for further seasoning. For a richer stew, add half and half or cream to the stew in place of some of the milk.

Pat Carver, Beals

Lobster and Corn Chowder

1 live lobster (about 1¹/₂ pounds)
4 cups half and half
4 tablespoons butter
2 medium potatoes, diced into ¹/₂-inch pieces
1 medium onion, minced
2 cups frozen corn kernels, thawed
¹/₈ teaspoon cayenne pepper
¹/₄ teaspoon salt
¹/₄ teaspoon ground black pepper

1. Boil, cool, and shell lobster, reserving the shells. Cut meat into 2-inch pieces.

2. Put the reserved lobster shells and carcass in a large saucepan with the half and half. Bring to a boil, lower the heat, and simmer for 4 minutes. Remove from heat and set aside.

3. Melt butter in a soup kettle; add potatoes, onion, and corn kernels, and sauté over medium-low heat until the onion is translucent.

4. Strain the lobster cream over the vegetables, and simmer slowly until the potatoes are tender. Stir in the lobster meat, cayenne pepper, salt, and black pepper. Simmer until lobster meat is hot, about 5 minutes.

Paula Colwell, Deer Isle

Do lobsters have teeth?
The teeth of a lobster are in its stomach. The stomach is located a very short distance from the mouth, and the food is actually chewed in the stomach between three grinding surfaces that look like molar teeth called the "gastric mill."

Lobster Stew

two 2-pound lobsters or four 1-pound lobsters
bay leaf
3 or 4 scallions with tops, finely chopped
$^2/_3$ cup butter
3 tablespoons flour
2 tablespoons fresh parsley, chopped
salt and pepper to taste
2 cups half and half
1 cup whole milk

1. Boil lobsters for 12 minutes in 1 quart of salted water with bay leaf added. Save broth and strain. Pick out lobster meat and cut into 1-inch pieces.

2. Sauté scallions in butter until tender. Make a roux by adding the flour to the scallion mix. Cook over low heat for 2 to 3 minutes. Add 1 cup broth, stirring constantly. Cook for 2 to 3 minutes more.

3. Add lobster meat and chopped parsley. Season with salt and pepper to taste.

4. Preheat mixture of half and half and whole milk in large saucepan. Add lobster mixture and stir until blended. Simmer over low heat for 30 minutes, but *do not allow it to boil*. Cool and refrigerate. Taste improves if the stew is allowed to set for a few hours or overnight.

Marie Snow, Yarmouth

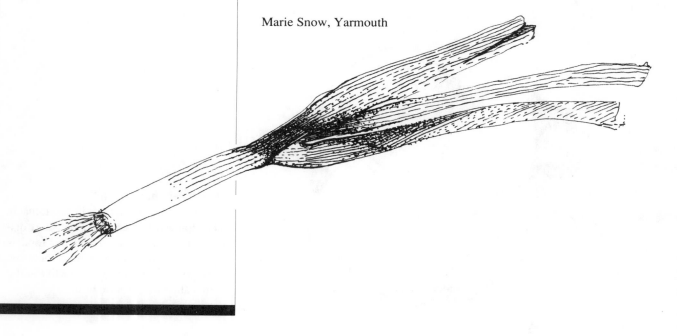

A Lobsterman's Stew

2 to 4 cups cooked lobster meat, cut into chunks
6 tablespoons butter
2 to 3 tablespoons sherry
1 can evaporated milk
4 cups whole milk

     1. Melt butter in a large saucepan or kettle. Add lobster meat and sauté until orange in color.

     2. Add sherry, stir, and cook a few minutes longer until slightly reduced.

     3. Add both kinds of milk and heat gently until warmed through, *never allowing it to boil*. Serve immediately, or let it set overnight and then reheat.

Gregory Griffin, Cape Elizabeth

Chilled Lobster Soup

shells from four $1^1/_2$ to 2-pound boiled lobsters (there is no meat in this—just the shells!)
$1^1/_2$ cups sherry
3 bay leaves
3 to 4 cups chicken stock
white pepper to taste
2 to 4 cups light cream
1 tablespoon fresh parsley, chopped

     1. Remove and discard eyes from lobster shells. Break or cut shells into 1-inch pieces, and break the legs at joints.

     2. Place shells in the smallest pot that will accommodate them, preferably a 2-quart pot. Add sherry, bay leaves, and enough chicken stock to cover. Season with pepper.

     3. Cover, and cook over low heat for 2 hours, stirring and mashing the shells frequently until the broth is flavorful and reddish-brown in color.

     4. Strain the soup and stir in the cream. Cover and refrigerate overnight. Before serving, whisk the soup and garnish it with chopped parsley.

Jean Hendrick, Deer Isle

A Lifelong Friend

I was going down to my camp on the island to work on my traps. When I got to the mooring, there was a little seal pup—just a little thing with his cord still on his belly—and the mother wasn't around. I went up beside him and pulled him over the side and put him in the bottom of the boat. He flopped all around and went up in the bow. But now, I thought, I got to find out what to do with him. So, I called Charles Beal—he's one of my good friends—and he said whatever you do, don't feed him, and get rid of him fast because you'll have a lifelong friend and you won't be able to get rid of him.
So I lowered him back over the side. Then I tied my boat on the mooring and started rowing ashore and he came right along with me. And that little seal stayed right around where I was working on the wharf. So, the only the thing I knew to do was to take him out to the one ledge where all the seals congregate and see if one of the mothers would adopt him. I took him out there and dropped him over the side by the ledge and said, "Well, good luck little fellow."

Earlon Beal, Beals (1990)

Lobsterman stringing bait

Lobster Quiche

one 10-inch pie shell
$^1/_2$ cup onions or scallions, finely chopped
2 tablespoons butter
$^1/_2$ teaspoon salt
$^1/_4$ teaspoon pepper
$1^1/_2$ cups cooked lobster meat, cut up
3 eggs
1 tablespoon tomato paste
2 cups medium cream
$^1/_4$ teaspoon nutmeg
2 tablespoons sherry
4 tablespoons Gruyere (or Swiss) cheese, shredded

1. Preheat oven to 400°.
2. Sauté onions, salt, and pepper in butter. Add lobster meat and set aside.
3. Beat eggs and mix in the tomato paste.
4. Scald the cream, add the nutmeg, and pour over the egg mixture. Add sherry and cheese.
5. Bake one 10-inch pie shell 8 minutes at 400°. Lower oven temperature to 350°. Arrange lobster meat on the bottom of the shell and pour the cream mixture over the lobster. Bake 30 to 40 minutes at 350° until filling is set.

Pat Poitras, Stonington

Lobster Quiche with Bacon

one 9-inch pie crust, unbaked
4 slices bacon
$1^1/_2$ to 2 cups lobster meat
$^1/_4$ cup scallions, sliced
1 cup Swiss cheese, shredded
3 eggs
$^1/_2$ cup milk
$^1/_2$ cup heavy cream
$^1/_2$ teaspoon salt
$^1/_8$ teaspoon pepper
dash of nutmeg

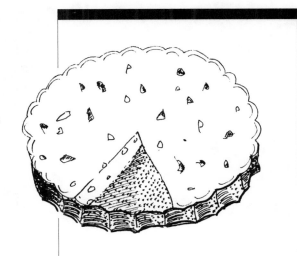

1. Preheat oven to 375°.
2. Line a quiche or pie pan with pie crust.
3. Cook bacon until crisp and set aside.
4. Layer half of the lobster meat, scallions, and Swiss cheese in pie crust. Repeat the process with remaining half.
5. Beat eggs and then add milk, cream, salt, pepper, and nutmeg. Pour over lobster mixture.
6. Crumble bacon into small pieces on top. Bake for 25 minutes until filling is set.

Sharon Blackmore, Deer Isle

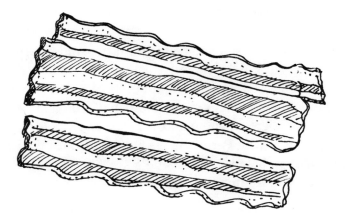

Follow The Leader
Georgie Pucker was in a rowboat and he came up to a ledge, and there was a whole bunch of sheep that got marooned out there. So, he rowed in and he was going to take two or three at a time to shore. Well, where one goes, they all go. They all got in the boat and left Georgie Pucker on the rock!

Rollins Kelley, Beals (1990)

Gilbert's dock, Pemaquid

Lobster Quiche Parmesan

one 9-inch pie shell, unbaked
2 cups cooked lobster meat
4 tablespoons butter
salt and pepper
3 tablespoons dry sherry
4 eggs
1 tablespoon flour
dash cayenne pepper
2 cups light cream
2 tablespoons Parmesan cheese, grated

1. Preheat oven to 375°.
2. Melt 3 tablespoons butter and sauté lobster lightly for 2 to 3 minutes.
3. Season with salt and pepper to taste. Add sherry, cover, and simmer 3 to 4 minutes.
4. Place lobster with the liquid in the pie shell.
5. Beat together eggs, flour, a pinch of salt, and cayenne pepper. Stir in the cream and pour over lobster.
6. Sprinkle with Parmesan cheese and drizzle with 1 tablespoon melted butter.
7. Bake for 40 minutes, or until custard is firm and crust is brown.

Connie Sullivan, Kittery

Lobster Crunch

1 can cream of mushroom soup
$^1\!/_2$ cup milk
2 cups cooked lobster meat, cut in pieces
2 eggs, hard-boiled and sliced
1 cup cooked peas
$^1\!/_2$ cup potato chips, chow mein noodles, or canned fried onion rings

    1. Preheat oven to 350°.
    2. Blend soup and milk in a 1-quart casserole. Stir in lobster meat, eggs, and peas. Bake for 20 minutes.
    3. Top with slightly crumbled potato chips, chow mein noodles, or fried onion rings. Bake for 5 minutes longer.

Harriet Heanssler, Deer Isle

New Harbor

How I Was Cured of Seasickness
I used to get carsick, seasick—I'd go on a merry-go-round and get seasick! Some days my father and I'd go outside and there'd be big swells and I'd plead with him to take me back. He'd drop me off at the wharf and I'd walk home.
One day my father said to me, "If you're going to go fishing, you've got to stick with it. I'll give you half of what we make today." I got to thinking about the money and what I'd do with it. And I went out and forgot to even think about being seasick. We came all the way up into the harbor and he looked at me and said, "Sam, you haven't been sick today, have you?" The minute he said that, I got the feeling and I looked around and I said to myself, "I can't get seasick. I'm right here in the harbor and it's flat calm!" And I've never been sick from that day on.

Richard Black, Bass Harbor (1990)

Whale of a Tale

There was a time over to Hurricane and it was a foggy morning, and in that double-ender I was pulling lobster traps and what came along out of the water but this great big whale. And he was much bigger than my double-ender, and my boat was 16 feet long. And I said, "There's just one thing for me to do to escape the whale and it's to get in shoal water as quick as I can." I was scared that he might come up under my boat. So, I rowed very fast and got in shoal water and said to myself, "Now I'll cross my oars and sit here and see if I can hear him blow again." Very shortly, I heard him blow and I was some happy—he was going way down to the southern end of Hurricane away from me.

Henry Walls, Vinalhaven (1973)
Northeast Archives #7710023

Lobster Stuffing for Peppers or Tomatoes

2 tablespoons butter
1/4 cup onion, chopped
3/4 cup celery, chopped
2 slices bacon, cooked and diced
1 cup soft bread crumbs
salt and pepper
1 cup cooked lobster meat, diced
2 eggs, beaten

1. Preheat oven to 350°.
2. Fry bacon bits on low heat until golden brown. Add onion, celery, and salt, and cook slowly until tender. Add bread crumbs and seasonings.
3. Combine lobster and beaten eggs, and add to first mixture. Stir to blend. Fill peppers or tomatoes and bake for about a half hour.

Harriet Bisset, Ellsworth

Lobster with Scallops and Mustard Sauce

1 or 2 lobsters, boiled, with meat removed
1 1/2 pounds fresh scallops
1 bay leaf
peppercorns
1/2 cup dry white wine
salt
1 cup mushrooms, sliced
2 tablespoons butter
1 tablespoon flour
1 heaping teaspoon of dry mustard
cayenne pepper
strained liquor from scallops
3/4 cup whole milk
baking scallop shells or ramekins

1. Put scallops in a pan with bay leaf, peppercorns,

wine, and salt, and bring slowly to a boil. Drain, reserve the liquid, and strain it.

2. Sauté mushrooms and add to the scallops.

· 3. Melt 1 tablespoon butter and stir in flour, mustard, salt, and cayenne pepper. Then pour this mixture into the strained liquor, thicken a little on low heat, and add milk.

4. Bring to a boil and add the lobster meat, which has been tossed in hot butter. Mix with the scallops and pour into shells or ramekins. Sprinkle with crumbs and grated cheese, dot with butter, and brown under the broiler.

Paula Colwell, Deer Isle

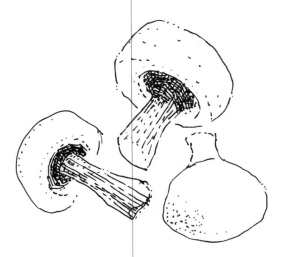

Creamed Lobster

3 tablespoons butter
1 cup cooked lobster meat, cut into pieces
2 tablespoons flour
1 cup light cream
salt, nutmeg, cayenne pepper, and lemon juice to taste
$1/2$ cup bread crumbs mixed with melted butter (optional)

1. Melt butter in a saucepan. Add lobster meat, cook and stir about 3 minutes.

2. Add flour and blend well. Slowly add cream and cook, stirring constantly, until well heated and thickened.

3. Season to taste with salt, nutmeg, cayenne pepper, and lemon juice.

4. Creamed lobster may be served as is or put in a buttered casserole. If you want to make a casserole, cover the creamed lobster with buttered crumbs and bake at 400° for approximately 10 minutes until the crumbs are brown.

Pat Poitras, Stonington

Sautéed Lobster

3 tablespoons butter
1 cup cooked lobster meat, cut up
fresh parsley, chopped (or dried)
salt and pepper to taste
$^1/_2$ teaspoon lemon juice

      1. Melt butter over low heat and add lobster meat. Sauté for 3 minutes.
      2. Sprinkle with chopped parsley, salt and pepper to taste, and lemon juice. Sauté approximately 5 minutes more until browned. Arrange on toast points. Serve with rice and tossed salad.

Serves 2 to 3.

Mabel Haskell, Stonington

Tangy Lobster

2 cups cooked lobster meat, cut into pieces
$^1/_3$ cup butter
1 teaspoon Worcestershire sauce
1 teaspoon dry mustard
1 tablespoon lemon juice

      1. Place all ingredients except lobster in a saucepan, and blend over low heat.
      2. Add lobster meat pieces and cook 6 minutes.

Serve on warm toast with a wedge of lemon.

Jane Alley, South Bristol

Washington County, 1981

*i*n Maine, lobster is usually least expensive in August, September, and October, the peak of the lobstering season. It's also the peak of the gardening season when fresh garden vegetables are available at every roadside stand and fill the markets. These hot summer days are the perfect time to have a lobster salad mixed with crisp lettuce, green beans, cucumbers, carrots, or tomatoes. Or you may just want to serve a traditional lobster roll, which always gets rave reviews.

Whatever you choose, we're sure you'll find that "quick and simple" does not have to mean uninteresting!

Chapter 4

QUICK & SIMPLE:

Salads and Sandwiches

King Neptune and Queen, Maine Seafoods Festival, 1965

Maine's Own Lobster Roll

2 cups cooked lobster meat, cut up and chilled
2 tablespoons mayonnaise
$\frac{1}{4}$ cup celery, finely diced

     1. Blend lobster meat with mayonnaise and add celery.
     2. Mix well and let stand in refrigerator until ready to use. Split and toast four hamburger or hot dog rolls and spread with melted butter. Rolls may also be buttered on the outside and grilled in a frying pan. Fill rolls with lobster mixture and serve.

Harriet Heanssler, Deer Isle

Castine, 1987

Sweet Mustard Sauce for Lobster

1 teaspoon prepared mustard
1 to $\frac{1}{2}$ teaspoon sugar to taste
4 teaspoons evaporated milk

     Mix all ingredients together and use as a spread for cut-up lobster meat on a roll.

Mrs. C. H. Beal, Beals; recipe handed down through several generations and given by Avery Kelley, Beals

Grandmother Hoppin's Salad

3 boiled lobsters
4 hard-boiled eggs
$\frac{1}{2}$ teaspoon salt
1 teaspoon dry mustard
3 tablespoons olive oil
$\frac{2}{3}$ cup vinegar
lettuce

     1. Remove meat from lobsters and chop into small pieces.

     2. Chop whites of eggs and mix with lobster meat.

     3. Put lobster tomalley in a bowl together with cooked egg yolks and mash with a tablespoon. Add salt, dry mustard, olive oil, and vinegar. Beat the dressing with an egg beater.

     4. Cover a large platter with lettuce leaves. Put lobster and egg white mixture over the lettuce and cover with dressing. Use small lobster claws around the edge of the platter for decoration. Chill in refrigerator before serving.

Grandmother Hoppin; recipe given by Jane Alley, South Bristol

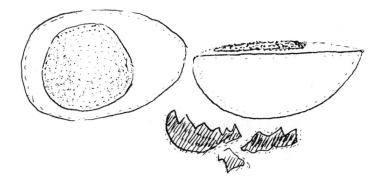

Glowing Claws

The town of York has a lobsterman with quite a sense of humor. He is always playing tricks on the other lobstermen.

One time he placed a pair of orange fluorescent vinyl work gloves on a large lobster and put it in another fellow's trap. Imagine the surprise on his friend's face when the trap came to the surface with the lobster reaching up with the gloves on.

Susan Smith, Kittery Point (1989)

What part of a lobster's body is measured to determine if it is large enough to keep?
A gauge is placed between the eye socket and the end of the large body shell, called the *carapace*, to measure the lobster.

Sea Goddess Feature, Department of Sea and Shore Fisheries, 1959

Lobster Salad with Egg and Celery

two 1^1/$_4$ pound lobsters, cooked and shelled
2 hard-boiled eggs, chopped
1 celery stalk, sliced
3 tablespoons mayonnaise
1 tablespoon milk
parsley, for garnish
lettuce leaves
1 lemon, sliced

    1. Cut lobster meat into bite-sized pieces and place in a bowl. Add hard-boiled eggs and celery.
    2. Mix together the mayonnaise and milk and add to the lobster mixture.
    3. If desired, put head and tail shells together, overlapping them slightly. Holding shells at an angle, fill with lobster salad, and garnish with parsley. Arrange on lettuce leaves and garnish with lemon slices.

Pat Carver, Beals

Quick and Simple Lobster Salad I

2 cups cooked lobster meat, cut into bite-sized pieces
1 small head lettuce, broken into bite-sized pieces
2 medium cucumbers, diced
1 small onion, diced
$^1/_2$ cup mayonnaise

     Mix all ingredients together. Serve on lettuce or as a sandwich filling.

Quick and Simple Lobster Salad II

2 cups cooked lobster meat, cut into bite-sized pieces
3 hard-boiled eggs, chopped
$^1/_4$ cup green olives, chopped
$^1/_3$ cup mayonnaise

     Mix all ingredients together. Serve chilled on lettuce or as a sandwich filling.

Donna Vachon, Stetson

Split Lobster Salad with Crabmeat

1 live lobster (1 to 1$^1/_2$ pounds)
lettuce leaves
bunch of watercress
1 cucumber, sliced
1 tomato, sliced
1 cup fresh crabmeat
mayonnaise

     1. Boil the lobster, split it down the center, and remove the dark vein. Leave the tail and claws attached to the lobster.
     2. Place the split lobster on lettuce leaves and watercress on a plate or platter. Arrange alternate slices of cucumber and tomato along the sides of the lobster.
     3. Place crabmeat on top of the split lobster. Serve cold with mayonnaise. This makes a very attractive presentation.

Mabel Haskell, Stonington

A Dirty Trick!
In the fall when the lobsters first shed, lobstermen have to measure each one when it looks like it might go the measure.* One time, a group of lobstermen got together and they saved snappers that just wouldn't go the measure, and they put 25 or 30 of them in this one trap and then they waited for my uncle to come along. They stood right there and watched him measure each one and throw it overboard, measure and throw it overboard—and he was getting madder every minute!

Richard Carver, Beals (1990)

* In Maine, lobsters have to be a certain length to be caught legally.

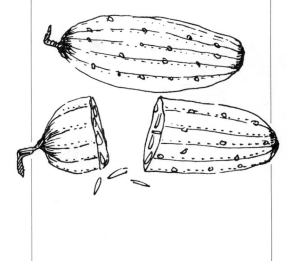

Lobster Salad with Green Aioli

3 medium potatoes, peeled and diced into $^1/_2$-inch pieces
$^3/_4$ pound fresh green beans, trimmed
salt and freshly ground black pepper
3 tablespoons olive oil
Meat from two $1^1/_2$ pound cooked lobsters

    1. Put the diced potatoes in a saucepan with cold water to cover. Bring water to a boil and simmer until potatoes are tender, about 6 minutes. Remove potatoes with a slotted spoon. Bring water back to a boil, add the beans, and boil until tender, about 7 minutes.
    2. Pat potatoes dry. In a heavy skillet, heat olive oil until almost smoking. Add potatoes to skillet and sauté, stirring frequently, until crisp and brown, about 10 minutes. Season with salt and pepper.
    3. Arrange lobster, beans, and potatoes on a serving plate and drizzle with aioli (see following recipe).

Aioli

2 small garlic cloves, minced
$^1/_3$ cup firmly packed parsley, stems removed, chopped
2 tablespoons lemon juice
1 egg yolk
$^1/_4$ teaspoon salt
$^1/_8$ teaspoon ground black pepper
4 tablespoons corn oil
6 tablespoons olive oil

    1. Mince garlic and parsley together by hand or in the work bowl of a food processor.
    2. Pour lemon juice into a small bowl or into the processor work bowl. Whisk or process in the egg yolk, parsley mixture, salt, and pepper until smooth.
    3. Combine the corn and olive oils and slowly whisk or process oils into the yolk mixture. This can be covered and refrigerated overnight.

Paula Colwell, Deer Isle

How far do lobsters travel?
Researchers have discovered that large lobsters travel great distances. Lobsters tagged in Maine have been found as far away as Massachusetts and Rhode Island.

"Old Salt"
Lobsters don't really travel a long ways in summer. Down in Stonington 10 or 12 years ago, there was a big lobster somebody caught down there. And they took an old coat and they made a sou'wester and a coat for him. They named him "Old Salt" and they caught him all over the place there. He only traveled two, three miles in a week.

Fishermen kept coming in, and they'd say "I caught Old Salt today." And the others would say, "Well, where did you throw him over?" And he'd tell them. And in two or three days someone else would catch Old Salt and he'd be only three or four miles from the place where he was last caught.

Mort Long, East Bluehill (1978)
Northeast Archives #1189026

Molded Lobster Loaf

4 cups cooked lobster meat, cut up
$^1/_2$ cup celery, diced
1 cup walnuts, chopped
1 teaspoon salt
$^1/_2$ teaspoon pepper
2 cups mayonnaise
5 hard-boiled eggs, chopped
1 cup stuffed green olives, sliced

     1. Combine all ingredients and press in a chilled mold.
     2. Chill overnight, unmold, and serve on lettuce. Garnish with olives.

Jane Alley, South Bristol

Lobster Aspic

8 ounces cream cheese, softened
2 tablespoons tomato paste
2 tablespoons gelatin
1 cup cold water
$^1/_4$ cup onion, chopped
$^1/_2$ cup green pepper, chopped
$^3/_4$ cup celery, chopped
1$^1/_2$ cups cooked lobster meat, chopped
1 cup mayonnaise
1 teaspoon Worcestershire sauce
salt and pepper to taste

     1. Combine softened cream cheese and tomato paste in a saucepan and heat.
     2. Soak the gelatin in water and add to the cheese mixture. Chill until partly congealed.
     3. Stir in onion, green peppper, celery, and lobster. Add mayonnaise and seasonings. Pour into a mold and chill until firm.

Jane Alley, South Bristol

Lobster and Shrimp Mousse

1 can cream of shrimp soup
8 ounces cream cheese
$^1/_4$ cup onion, chopped
1 cup Miracle Whip or mayonnaise
2 tablespoons gelatin, softened in 1 cup cold water
1 cup cooked lobster meat, finely chopped
1 cup celery, chopped

     1. Heat together the shrimp soup, cream cheese, and onion.
     2. Blend in the Miracle Whip or mayonnaise and gelatin.
     3. Add the lobster meat and celery. Pour into a 6-cup mold and chill until firm.

Paula Colwell, Deer Isle

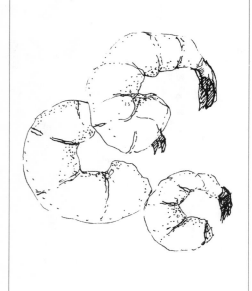

Layered Lobster Salad

2 cups lettuce, shredded
$^1/_4$ cup green onions, finely chopped
1 cup celery, thinly sliced
1 cup carrots, coarsely grated
1 cup frozen peas, thawed
2 cups cooked lobster meat, cut into pieces

Dressing
$^1/_2$ cup mozzarella cheese, grated
$^2/_3$ cup natural yogurt
$^1/_2$ cup mayonnaise
1 tablespoon lemon juice
2 teaspoons honey
1 tablespoon chives, finely chopped
$^1/_4$ teaspoon dill weed
2 tablespoons bacon bits
1 small clove garlic, crushed
$^1/_4$ cup Parmesan cheese, grated

    1. In a glass bowl, layer lettuce, onions, celery, carrots, peas, and lobster meat. Refrigerate for several hours.
    2. Combine ingredients for dressing and serve with the salad.

Harriet Heanssler, Deer Isle

Bass Harbor, 1987

Flying Lobsters!
The exhaust pipe of the boat used to be pumped out through the side. Well, just before we got to Bertie Smith, Lester stuffed a lobster into that exhaust pipe. Bertie always came up alongside to talk for awhile and when he came right up in range of that pipe, Lester pulled the throttle open and that lobster shot right out and just missed Bertie!

Earlon Beal, Beals (1990)

Easy Lobster Filling for Chilled Tomatoes

1 cup cooked lobster meat, cut into small pieces
$^1/_2$ cup celery or peeled cucumber, finely chopped
$^1/_2$ cup mayonnaise
2 teaspoons lemon juice
paprika

Mix all ingredients (except paprika) together and stuff a tomato shell. Sprinkle the top with paprika.

Harriet Bisset, Ellsworth

Lobster and Macaroni Salad

$1/2$ pound elbow or shell macaroni
$1/2$ cup mayonnaise
$3/4$ cup milk
$1/2$ cup French dressing
$1/2$ teaspoon salt
$1/4$ teaspoon pepper
1 cup cooked lobster meat, cut into pieces
1 cup celery, thinly sliced
2 small white onions, thinly sliced
3 hard-boiled eggs, sliced
2 cups cabbage, shredded

    1. Cook macaroni according to package directions, drain, and put in refrigerator to chill.
    2. In a large bowl, combine mayonnaise, milk, French dressing, salt, and pepper. Add chilled macaroni and toss.
    3. Add lobster meat and remaining ingredients. Toss and chill.

Pat Poitras, Stonington

Calvin Hale and Gardner Gross (at wheel), Stonington, 1984

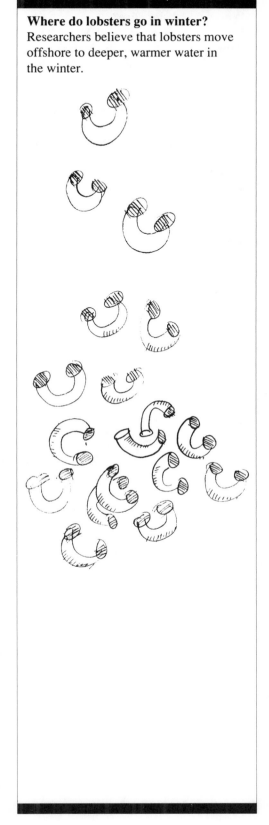

Where do lobsters go in winter?
Researchers believe that lobsters move offshore to deeper, warmer water in the winter.

Where do lobsters live?

Studies at the University of Maine have shown that lobsters are very choosy where they live. Small lobsters (less than $1^1/_2$" carapace length) live mainly in shallow water where there is a small rock or "cobble" bottom; adolescent lobsters ($1^1/_2$" to $3^1/_2$" CL) live where there are larger boulders; and reproductive, adult size lobsters usually inhabit deeper water. It has been observed that lobsters of all ages often dig burrows and live in crevices.

Hot Lobster Sandwich

1 package Pillsbury crescent rolls
4 ounces whipped cream cheese with chives
1 cup cooked lobster meat, chopped
$^1/_4$ cup cheddar cheese, shredded

    1. Preheat oven to 350°.

    2. Unroll dough and pinch the precut lines together. Fold dough in half and roll out to approximately 9x12-inch rectangle.

    3. Down the long side, spread three-quarters of the cream cheese. Top with lobster and sprinkle with cheddar cheese.

    4. Roll up jelly roll-style and place on ungreased cookie sheet, seam side down. Pinch and turn under the ends. Bake for 10 to 15 minutes or until brown. Cut into slices to serve. This is also delicious served cold.

Kathy Brazer, Ogunquit

*l*obster bakes have been a summer tradition on the Maine coast since the beginning of the 1900's. Many Mainers feel that this is absolutely the best way to eat lobsters! Cooked on the beach in the fresh salt air and steamed in seaweed, lobsters just seem to capture the true flavor of the ocean.

Of course, to have an authentic lobster bake, the ceremony is just as important as the food. Besides lobster, you have to have fresh Maine clams, corn on the cob, potatoes, onions, and hard-boiled eggs, and then stack them in the right order in the pile of seaweed so everything comes out done to perfection. Once you've eaten a Maine lobster bake, you'll understand why this is one of those traditions that will never die.

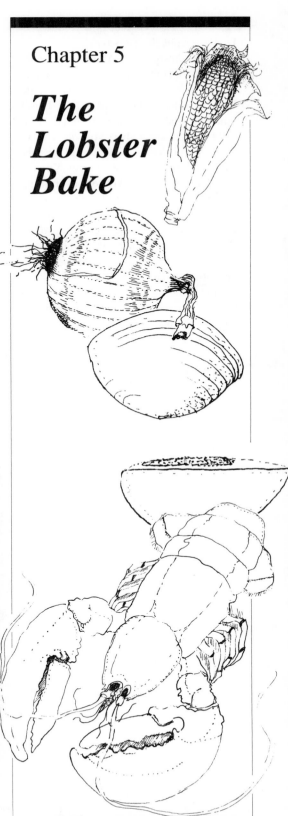

Chapter 5

The Lobster Bake

Lobster bake at Sebasco

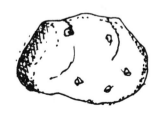

Don't Forget the Lobsters!

The other day my sister Martha and I were talking about our family clambakes which we had at least once a summer on Granite Point in Biddeford Pool. She said, "Don't you remember the time we forgot the lobsters?" You see, when you do a trash barrel clambake, you always put the lobsters on the bottom of the barrel. You eat the clams first, then you eat everything else except the lobsters at the same time. The grand finale is always the lobsters and everyone looks forward to eating them. Well, when we got to the bottom, we discovered that we'd forgotten to put in the lobsters. They were all still jumping around in the back of the truck! We had to take them in the house and boil them on the top of the electric stove. They just didn't seem to taste quite as good.

Lisa Larrabee Werner,
Cape Elizabeth (1990)

Eating lobsters at Gilbert's, Pemaquid

Eating lobsters at Maine Seafoods Festival, Rockland, 1965

The Trash Barrel Clambake

1 new or clean 30-gallon galvanized barrel with cover
3 or 4 large onion bags
1 bushel seaweed (wet)
2 armfuls of split, dry hardwood

     1. On the beach, set up rocks or cement blocks to rest the barrel on, allowing plenty of room underneath for fire. Put about 4 inches of seawater in the barrel and set it on the fire. After water boils hard, add some seaweed and get it boiling hard again.
     2. Add food all at one time: lobsters in a bag on bottom, layer of seaweed, then bag of onions and potatoes, another layer of seaweed, then bag of corn, more seaweed, and lastly, a bag of clams with seaweed on top. Put a little seaweed around the bags to keep them away from the side of the can. Cover with the lid. (Potatoes and onions need no prior cooking but try to have them all the same size. Leave some of the husks on the corn.)
     3. Keep the fire blazing hard all the while and in about 25 minutes the clams will be done and open up. When the clams are done, take them out to eat, tip over the barrel and leave it (keeping it out of the sand) until you've eaten the clams.

Paul Larrabee, Gorham

Left to right: (back row) Paul Johnston, Albert Springer, Francis Phippen; (front row) Margie Clarke Ackerman, Phoebe Clarke Johnston, Hancock, late 1940s

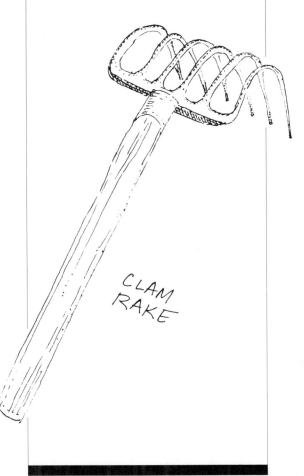

CLAM RAKE

A Big Appetite!

Once someone asked Uncle Eben why he was called "uncle" and he said, "Because I'm an uncle to just about everybody." He'd usually eat about five suppers a night because he'd know when people were eating and he'd stop by!

One day, a bunch of fishermen were off to the island lobstering and they were going to sail into Beals for provisions. Back in those days they had row pods and they could sail in with the sou'west winds after they hauled their traps. That morning they'd saved a lot of short lobsters and they gave them to Uncle Eben (who was sort of the cook) to make a lobster stew so they'd have it when they came back to the island. Uncle Eben was boiling the lobsters when they hauled off and then took them down on the rocks to cool. He took a look and saw a boat coming and he thought it was the warden. So Uncle Eben decided the best way to get rid of the lobsters was to eat them up. So the guys came back and said, "Uncle Eben, where's the lobsters?" "Well, Godfrey mighty dear, I saw a boat coming and it looked like the warden and I ate them." They never did know what happened to the shells!

Avery Kelley, Beals (1990)

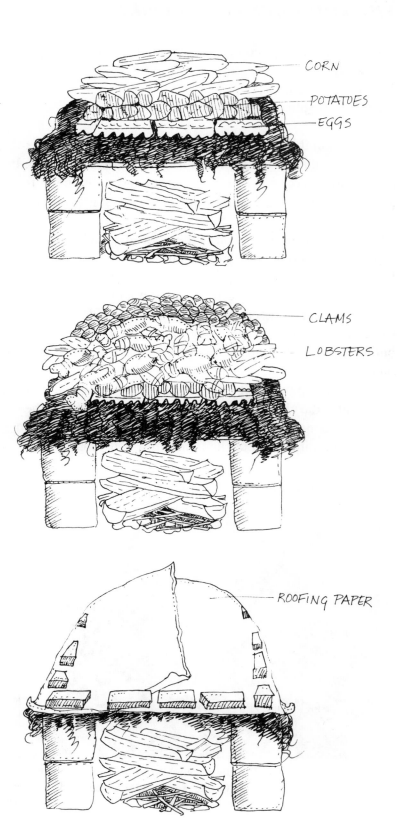

CORN

POTATOES

EGGS

CLAMS

LOBSTERS

ROOFING PAPER

Alleys' Traditional Maine Lobster Bake

1. Build a fireplace by piling up cinder blocks 2 rows high to form the base. Place an iron on top to make a table. Sometimes we flatten an old fuel tank for the iron. The size depends on the number of people. For 30 to 100 people, you need an iron that is approximately 4'x6'.

2. Place a layer of seaweed, at least 6 inches thick, on top of the iron.

3. Put eggs in cardboard (not styrofoam) cartons with holes poked in the bottom and place them on top of the seaweed in the center.

4. Place potatoes (that have been cleaned and wrapped in foil) and onions (peeled and wrapped in foil) on top of the eggs.

5. Place corn (partially husked and some silk removed) on top of potatoes, onions, and eggs.

6. Using untarred roofing paper, cover the back of the bake and hold in place with rocks or bricks. Have someone hold the paper up in the front while lobsters and clams are added.

7. Mound the lobsters on top of the corn. Then, mound the clams on top of the lobsters. The juice from the clams and lobsters cooks the potatoes, onions, and corn.

8. Lower the paper attached at the back over the clams. Add another sheet of paper to cover the front and one more length of paper to cover the seam.

9. Cover the whole bake with at least 6 inches of fresh seaweed.

10. Light the fire and cook 45 to 60 minutes. A good way to tell if everything is done is when the juice stops running off the iron.

11. When "picking the bake," watch out because everything will be very hot.

Lewis Alley, South Bristol (recipe handed down from Ambrose to Ernest to Lewis Alley)

Where There's Smoke, There's Bound To Be...

One time Lewis and I had a clambake for the Youth Fellowship. We were down at the shore having our clambake which produces a lot of smoke. We noticed that the local volunteer fire chief Joe Gamage and his volunteers were rushing around the dirt roads on the island frantically looking for a house that was on fire. We were just sitting on the rocks watching the guys run all around us. Then they discovered that the smoke was just us having a clambake. So they came down and ate with us.

Jane Alley, South Bristol (1990)

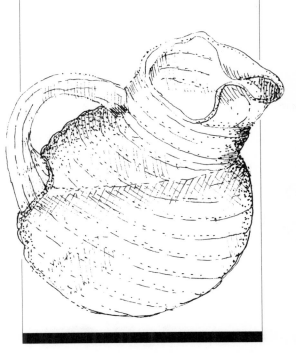

Lobsters Aplenty!
When I was a kid, my father'd take the whole family on picnics and he'd take a little dip net and go around the rocks and dip up lobsters enough for our dinner—just like you do in the pound! He told us there were so many lobsters, they used to use them for fertilizer to put on the fields.

Rollins Kelley, Beals (1990)

Etta and Walter Clarke, Hancock, c. 1910

Clarke family "shore picnic," Hancock, 1944

A Hancock Shore Dinner

When I was growing up in Hancock, we never went on a "lobster bake." We went on shore picnics down by the bay, which usually meant lobsters, clams, and corn-on-the-cob. But we never called such events "bakes." When we were being fancy, we called them "shore dinners."

Oftentimes the lobsters were boiled in seawater in a kettle; sometimes they were "baked" in seaweed. As a kid, I enjoyed sucking the meat and juice out of the lobster legs and spreading the tomalley on crackers. One of my aunts used to say tomalley was just as good as caviar.

The Hancock peninsula doesn't have much for beaches, so we'd have to find a good spot on a ledge or on the bank of the shore on which to balance ourselves and our picnic. One of my aunts from New York used to bring her wind-up Victrola so we could have music while we ate. The menfolk usually took care of the cooking of the lobsters and clams while the women were in charge of the salad (usually potato), melted butter, rolls, desserts, drinks, and utensils. While the adults were busily preparing the repast, the kids would be swimming and skimming rocks off the water; and if it was low tide, digging and squishing about the clamflats, playing with seaweed, and hunting for crabs and jellyfish.

Sanford Phippen, Orono (1990); author of *The Police Know Everything, People Trying to be Good, Cheap Gossip,* and editor of *The Best Maine Stories*

Eastern States Royalty Prince Stephen Shaw and Princess Susan Bunnell tackle eating a lobster. They were guests of Governor John H. Reed at a coastal lobster festival.

What is a lobster pound? A lobster car?
Live lobsters are held (and fed) in saltwater storage areas called *pounds* until they are sold. Lobsters are penned in by fences or dams, which let the water in but keep the lobsters from swimming out. Lobstermen also store their catch in floating wooden containers called *live cars* while they wait for the prices to rise before selling the lobsters.

Conary Cove Lobster Pound, Deer Isle, 1987

Hermon Conary (great uncle of Basil Heanssler, owner of Conary Cove Lobster Pound), Deer Isle, c. 1928

Conary Cove Lobster Pound, Deer Isle, 1987

*e*very experienced cook knows that the most successful meals delight the eye as well as the palate. For all the recipes in this chapter, the bright red shell of the cooked lobster is an important part of the presentation. When red is contrasted with the vivid yellow of a fresh lemon and the dark green of parsley sprigs, this is one of the most attractive ways to serve lobster.

For several of the recipes in this chapter, you need to split a live lobster. For complete instructions on how to do this, please consult "Basics: How to Start."

Chapter 6

Broiled, Baked, & Stuffed

Couple looking delighted with broiled lobster dinner, Department of Economic Development (now Maine State Planning Office), c. 1950

Broiled Lobster

1 small (1-pound) or half a large (1³/₄- to 2¹/₄-pound) live
lobster per serving
butter or margarine, melted
lemon wedges, for garnish
parsley sprigs, for garnish (optional)

     1. Place the lobster on its back. Holding the head, insert
the point of a sharp knife just under the mouth and quickly
bring the knife down the body.
     2. With both hands, crack the body of the lobster open,
splitting it in half.
     3. Remove the dark vein from the tail. Leave the light
green tomalley and the dark roe.
     4. With a hammer or lobster cracker, crack the large part
of each large claw.
     5. Place the lobster, cut side up, on a rack in a broiling
pan. Brush meat with melted butter. Broil 7 to 9 inches from
the heat source. Do not turn it over.
     6. Brush occasionally with melted butter during cook-
ing. Lobster is cooked when the shell is red, about 8 to 15
minutes. Place on a plate and garnish with lemon wedges and
parsley. Serve with more butter.

Pat Carver, Beals

NET MENDING
TOOL

How long have lobsters been fished in Maine?
There are reports of lobsters caught in
1605 when early explorers threw a net
over the side of a boat to catch them. The
commercial lobster fishery began around
the mid-1800s.

Lewis Alley, South Bristol, c. 1970

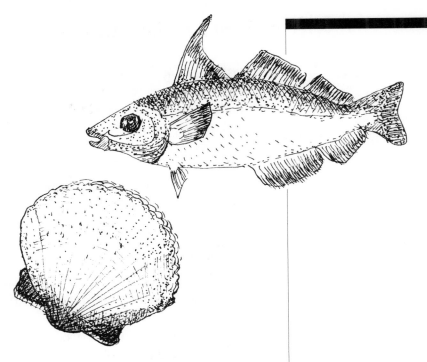

Jasper's Baked Stuffed Maine Lobster

1 live lobster, about 1 to 1¹/₂ pounds
1 egg
3 ounces (about ¹/₂ cup) Ritz cracker crumbs
1 tablespoon Parmesan cheese, grated
¹/₂ stick butter, melted
1 ounce scallops
2 ounces shrimp
3 ounces haddock

Recipe is for stuffing one lobster. Multiply ingredient amounts by number of lobsters.

1. Preheat oven to 450°.
2. Split live lobsters with a sharp, pointed knife from head to tail. Open flat and remove intestinal vein, stomach, and tomalley. If desired, save tomalley to add to stuffing. Crack claws, remove meat, and cut into pieces.
3. Moisten crumbs with butter and egg. Then add Parmesan cheese, tomalley and fresh raw seafood. Spread stuffing mixture generously in cavity, and split tail.
4. Place on cookie sheet and bake for 20 minutes.

Fred Graham, Jasper's Restaurant and Motel, Ellsworth

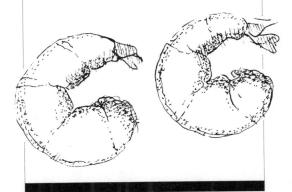

Chet's Baked Stuffed Lobster

4 large 2-pound live lobsters
1 stack saltine crackers, finely crushed
tomalley from lobster bodies
1 stick butter, melted
2 tablespoons Worcestershire sauce

1. Place lobsters in boiling, salted water and boil for 10 minutes. Pour off hot water and cool in a cold water rinse. Break off the claws and pick out the meat. Cut the lobster meat into pieces.

2. Preheat oven to 350°.

3. Place lobsters on their backs in a large pan. Slit each one down the length of its body to make a cavity for the stuffing.

4. Remove tomalley from the body and place in a large bowl. Remove the vein from the tail and discard.

5. Combine the remaining ingredients with tomalley to make the stuffing.

6. Place claw and knuckle meat in the cavity and fill the cavity with stuffing. Bake for 45 minutes.

Chet Rittall, Boothbay

What is a lobster "smack"?
A boat that carries live lobsters in seawater.

Two-masted schooner smacks at A.C. McLoon Lobster Co. wharf, 1915

Curried Stuffed Lobsters

4 cooked lobsters
2 tablespoons butter
2 tablespoons flour
1 tablespoon curry powder
1 cup milk
1¼ cups heavy cream
salt to taste, if desired
freshly ground black pepper
1⅓ cups cooked rice

1. Preheat oven to 400°.
2. Remove the large lobster claws. Crack the claws and remove the meat. Cut the meat into bite-sized pieces. Set aside in a bowl.
3. Cut the small feelers from the lobsters and put them in a bowl. Split each lobster in half lengthwise. Discard the small, tough sac near the eyes. Remove the soft coral and tomalley and add them to the bowl with the feelers. Set aside.
4. Remove the tail meat from the lobsters. Cut it into bite-sized medallions. Add the medallions to the bowl with the claw meat. Set aside.
5. Arrange the lobster shells split-side-up on a baking sheet.
6. Melt the butter in a saucepan and add the flour and curry powder, stirring with a wire whisk. Add the milk, continuing to stir with the whisk.
7. Scrape the coral and tomalley along with the feelers into the container of a food processor. Blend until smooth with some lumps. Pour and scrape the mixture into a sieve, pressing it through with a wooden spoon to extract as much liquid from the solids as possible. Add this to the curry sauce, stirring. Discard the solids. Add salt and pepper to taste.
8. Spoon equal portions of the rice into each lobster shell. Add equal portions of the lobster meat. Spoon enough curry sauce over the top of each serving to cover. The remaining sauce will be served on the side.
9. Place the lobsters in the oven and bake for about 5 minutes until piping hot. Serve the stuffed lobster halves with the remaining heated curry sauce on the side.

Paula Colwell, Deer Isle

Is lobster blood red?
Lobster blood is usually a gray or slightly blue color, but it can sometimes be orange, green, or light pink.

The smack *Silas McLoon*, built in 1913 in East Boothbay, carried 18,000 pounds of lobsters.

In the Lobster Smack Days

Back in the old days, lobstermen sold their catch to "smacks" that came around to some of the coastal Maine islands. A smack was a vessel usually about 60 feet long with a hold where the lobsters were stored, filled with seawater. The water was circulated by the movement of the boat.

It was the custom for the fishermen to dump their lobsters on the deck of the smack. Then the captain would take his toe and push the lobsters into the hold, counting each one as he did so. At this particular time, lobsters were being sold for 2 cents each.

The captain of this particular smack was a man by the name of Mr. Partridge. After watching the captain push the lobsters into the hold for some time, Grandfather commented, "Count as often as you can, Mr. Partridge."

Ed Blackmore, Stonington (1989)

Baked Stuffed Lobster with Crabmeat Stuffing

six 1¹/₂-pound live lobsters
1¹/₂ sticks butter
1 medium pepper, finely cut
2 cups crabmeat
1³/₄ cups seasoned bread crumbs
2 to 3 teaspoons lemon juice
¹/₄ cup Parmesan cheese, grated
1 tablespoon parsley, chopped
¹/₂ cup cooking sherry
milk or cream (as needed)

1. Preheat oven to 425°.
2. Melt butter and sauté the green pepper over low heat.
3. Combine the crabmeat and seasoned bread crumbs and mix in sautéed peppers.
4. Add lemon juice, Parmesan cheese, parsley, sherry, and enough milk or cream to obtain desired consistency.
5. Split six live lobsters with a sharp, pointed knife from head to tail. Open lobster flat and remove the intestinal vein and tomalley. Leave the claws attached.
6. Stuff the lobsters with dressing and sprinkle with grated cheese, if desired.
7. Place lobsters on cookie sheets. Brush claws and sides of lobsters with a little olive oil. Bake for at least 40 minutes.

Sally Haskell, Stonington

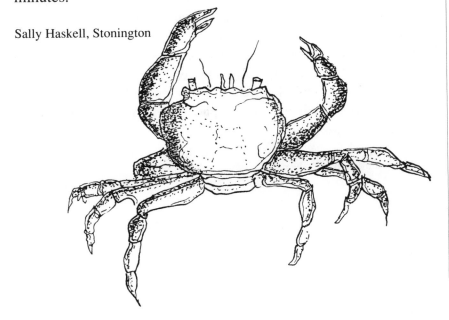

What color are lobsters?
The American lobster is usually greenish brown or blackish orange when alive. However, lobsters also come in blue, yellow, red, and white. Except for the white ones, they all turn red when cooked.

Chameleon Lobsters?
There were two school teachers, spinsters they say, about fifty or fifty-five. And they used to come here every year for quite awhile. One day they came hurrying up to a lobsterman and they said, "We've just seen a blue lobster down at the lobster pound. And we've asked everyone, but none of them can tell us how that lobster came to be blue."
"Well," says the lobsterman, "that was probably a lobster that had laid alongside of a blue rock and changed color."
And they went off all happy because they'd found out why that lobster was blue.

Ralph Phippen, Southwest Harbor (1967)
Northeast Archives #30237

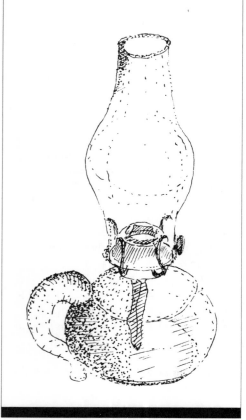

Baked Stuffed Lobster Tails with Newburg Sauce

4 lobsters, boiled and cooled
4 tablespoons butter
2 heaping tablespoons flour
$1^1/_4$ cups milk
$^1/_4$ cup plus 1 tablespoon dry white wine or sherry
$^1/_2$ teaspoon paprika
salt to taste
8 Ritz crackers
8 saltine crackers
1 teaspoon Worcestershire sauce

Newburg Sauce

1. Melt 2 tablespoons of the butter over low heat and make a roux by adding the flour. Stir until blended.

2. Add paprika, milk, and $^1/_4$ cup of wine or sherry. Cook until thick, stirring constantly. If too thick, add a little more wine and milk. It should be the consistency of a medium white sauce.

3. Cut up lobster meat from claws, joints, and body, and add to the sauce. Salt to taste and set aside.

Stuffed Tails

1. Preheat oven to 350°.

2. Break tails from cooked lobster. To remove the vein cut down center of inside of tail through to back shell, being careful not to cut back shell. Spread tail cavity apart and fill with Newburg sauce.

3. Top with a mixture of Ritz and saltine cracker crumbs, 2 tablespoons of melted butter, Worcestershire sauce, and 1 tablespoon of white wine.

4. Bake tails in a baking pan until lightly browned and heated through.

Shirley James, Milbridge

Lobster Diablo

four 1¼-pound live lobsters
2 to 3 tablespoons butter
3 tablespoons olive oil
1 tablespoon garlic, chopped
1 large can whole tomatoes, finely chopped
½ teaspoon whole leaf oregano
1 tablespoon fresh parsley, chopped
¼ teaspoon Tabasco sauce

    1. Preheat oven to 350°.
    2. Boil lobsters, cool, and pick out the meat. Cut meat into bite-sized pieces. Reserve body cavity shells.
    3. Sauté lobster meat in butter and drain.
    4. Sauté garlic in olive oil. Add tomatoes, parsley, oregano, and Tabasco sauce and sauté a few more minutes. Add lobster meat.
    5. Split lobster body shells by cutting halfway through them from top to bottom.
    6. Put the mixture into the body shells. Bake for 10 to 14 minutes.

Barry Johnston, Fisherman's Wharf, Boothbay Harbor

Captain Charles Dodge and his daughter on smack *Consolidated*, 1928

My First Trip on a Smack
My first trip on a lobster smack was, I believe, in 1947. They were taking the smack *Pauline McLoon*, which was a little double-ended smack. It was in the winter and it was cold, and it seemed like I was going to Europe. We just went from here to South Hancock which is up in the Skillins River in Sullivan.

Avery Kelley, Beals (1990)

A Matter of Location
It was a beautiful summer day in August and grandfather was busily at work hauling his lobster traps in lower Penobscot Bay in an area of much shoal water and kelps that reach to the surface. Anyone not familiar with the area would want to be very sure of the water depth before attempting passage. Grandfather looked up to see a very nice sailboat approaching, hove to, and the captain asked grandfather, "How much water do we have here?" Grandfather's reply was,"There's plenty of water here. All you got to do is stay in it!"

Ed Blackmore, Stonington (1989)

Ed Blackmore, President of Maine Lobstermen's Association, with sternman Curt Haskell, 1971

*f*or these combinations, you can use just the meat from the lobster's tail or claws. Or, if you are like many lobster lovers in Maine, you may also want to pick out all the meat from the body. Either way, this chapter will give you many suggestions for delicious ways to combine cooked lobster meat with vegetables, grains, pasta, and other seafoods for a hearty, wholesome meal.

Chapter 7

Zesty Combina-tions:

Casseroles

Islesford, 1988

Lobster Casserole with Water Chestnuts and Bacon

1 to 2 cups cooked lobster meat
$^1/_4$ cup onion, finely chopped
1 green pepper, finely chopped
6 to 8 fresh mushrooms, sliced
1 can water chestnuts, sliced
$^1/_2$ cup sherry
1 egg yolk
$^1/_2$ cup all-purpose cream
1 teaspoon dry mustard
1 cup mayonnaise
1 cup cheddar cheese, grated
2 to 3 slices bacon, cooked and crumbled

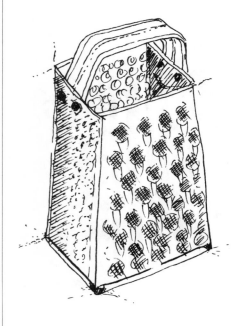

1. Preheat oven to 350°.

2. Place lobster meat, onion, pepper, mushrooms, water chestnuts, and sherry in a frying pan. Bring to a boil and cook until vegetables are just tender. Spoon mixture into a casserole.

3. Combine egg yolk and cream in a saucepan and cook slightly. Then cool, and add mustard and mayonnaise. Combine with casserole mixture.

4. Top with grated cheese. Bake for 15 to 20 minutes. Remove from oven and sprinkle with crumbled bacon.

Kathy Brazer, Ogunquit

Lobster and Artichoke Casserole

1 tablespoon butter
$^1/_2$ cup celery, chopped
1 small green pepper, chopped
1 medium onion, chopped
$1^1/_2$ cups cooked lobster meat, cut in bite-sized chunks
$8^1/_2$ ounce can artichoke hearts (not marinated), cut into thirds
1 teaspoon lemon juice
$^1/_2$ teaspoon dill
1 cup cheddar cheese, grated
Parmesan cheese, grated

    1. Sauté celery, green pepper and onion in butter. When translucent, add lobster, artichoke hearts, lemon juice, and dill. Just warm and remove from heat.
    2. Spoon mixture into casserole dish and cover with cheese. Set aside and make a white sauce.

White sauce
2 tablespoons butter
2 tablespoons flour
salt and pepper
1 cup milk

    1. Preheat oven to 350°.
    2. Melt butter in a saucepan. Stir in flour, salt, and pepper. Add milk, stirring constantly until thickened.
    3. Pour the white sauce over the casserole mixture and sprinkle with Parmesan cheese. Bake approximately 30 minutes.

Kathy Brazer, Ogunquit

Better Late Than Never!
Ben lived out on Cranberry Island when I was a boy. He must have been about old enough to be my grandfather. And every year or two, Ben'd just take off, without telling anyone, and go to sea for a year or so. And then he'd just turn up again. One day he said to his wife, "Bell, I guess I'll go up to Southwest Harbor. Anything you want?"
And she said, "Yes. Why don't you get me some molasses? Here's the jug." And he took off for Southwest Harbor with the jug under his arm. And just a year later, to the day, he walked into the kitchen out there on Cranberry, and banged the jug on the table and said, "There Bell, there's your molasses!"

Anonymous (1967)
Northeast Archives #30223

Lobster Thermidor

4 tablespoons butter
$1/4$ cup green onions, chopped
4 tablespoons flour
1 teaspoon dry mustard
$1^{1}/_{2}$ cups light cream
1 tablespoon parsley, minced
1 teaspoon dried tarragon, crushed
$1/2$ teaspoon salt
$1/8$ teaspoon pepper
$1/2$ cup cooking sherry
2 cups cooked lobster meat, cut into chunks
$1/4$ cup Parmesan cheese, grated

    1. Preheat oven to 400°.
    2. Melt butter in medium-sized saucepan and sauté onions. Blend in flour and mustard.
    3. Add cream and cook, stirring constantly, until mixture thickens. Stir in parsley, tarragon, salt, pepper, and sherry. Blend until smooth.
    4. Add lobster meat to the sauce. Place the mixture in a shallow baking dish and sprinkle with cheese. Bake for 15 to 20 minutes or until bubbly and lightly browned.

Madge Kelly, Sedgwick

How long does it take for a lobster to grow to one pound in weight?
It takes four to seven years.

Lobster Thermidor in Pastry Shells

lobster bisque (see recipe below)
puff pastry shells
parsley and paprika for garnish

1. Use the recipe below for bisque.
2. Serve over a puff pastry shell and garnish with a claw, parsley, and paprika. This can be used as a main course or as an appetizer in small-sized shells.

Lobster Bisque
meat from 10 to 15 lobsters, reserving enough claws for garnish
1 stick butter (*not* margarine)
$^1/_2$ cup flour
paprika
6 cups stock (see recipe below)
2 cups cream
$^1/_4$ cup sherry
salt and pepper

1. Melt butter, and add flour and paprika. Slowly blend in the stock and simmer for 5 minutes.
2. Add the lobster meat. This bisque tastes best if done the day ahead and then refrigerated until it is just about time to serve. When ready to serve, heat to a simmer, remove from the heat, and add the cream, sherry, salt, and pepper. You may want to add a little water if it is too thick or too pungent.

Lobster Stock
ten to fifteen 1-pound lobsters
1 onion
several stalks of celery

1. Boil lobsters and save the water you boiled them in. Shell the lobsters and save all shells and bodies. Break them up into big pieces and put into the lobster water.
2. Cut up the onion and celery into large pieces and add to the pot. Boil for 2 to 3 hours.
3. Strain out the shells, bodies, and vegetables. Boil until reduced to about 6 cups.

Tudor Austin, Kittery Point

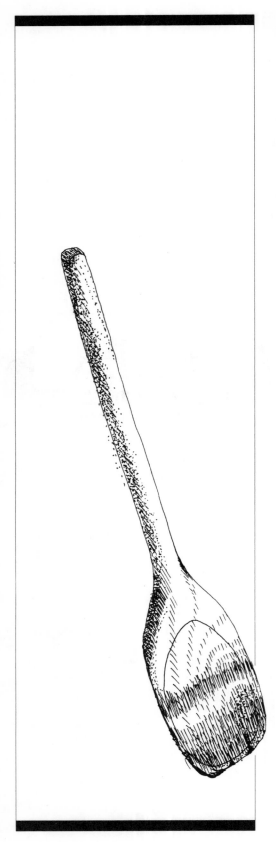

Lobster Casserole

2 to 3 cups cooked lobster meat, cut into bite-sized pieces
6 tablespoons butter
4 tablespoons flour
$^3/_4$ teaspoon dry mustard
salt and paprika to taste
6 to 8 slices bread, crusts removed
2 cups medium cream
1 tablespoon sherry
cracker crumbs, finely crushed

     1. Preheat oven to 350°.
     2. Sauté lobster in 2 tablespoons of the butter.
     3. Melt 4 tablespoons butter and add flour to make a roux.
     4. Stir in half of the cream and heat slowly to make a sauce. Add salt, paprika, and dry mustard.
     5. Break bread into small pieces and mix with the sauce. Add remainder of cream and sherry.
     6. Turn into buttered casserole and top with cracker crumbs, lightly browned in butter. Bake for 30 minutes. For full flavor, this should be made at least 4 or 5 hours before baking.

Donna Vachon, Stetson

Lobster Harpin

4 cups cooked lobster meat, cut up
1 tablespoon lemon juice
3 tablespoons salad oil
$^3/_4$ cup uncooked rice
2 tablespoons margarine
$^1/_4$ cup green pepper, chopped
$^1/_4$ cup onion, minced
1 teaspoon salt
$^1/_8$ teaspoon pepper
$^1/_8$ teaspoon mace
dash cayenne pepper
1 can tomato soup, undiluted

1 cup cream or half and half
$3/4$ cup slivered almonds

     1. Toss lobster meat with lemon juice and salad oil. Refrigerate.
     2. Cook rice and refrigerate.
     3. Preheat oven to 350°.
     4. Sauté green pepper and onion in margarine. Add to rice and lobster meat, along with the other ingredients. Save $1/4$ cup of the nuts and some lobster meat to put on top.
     5. Bake for 35 minutes. Top with remaining nuts and lobster and bake 20 minutes longer.

Harriet Heanssler, Deer Isle

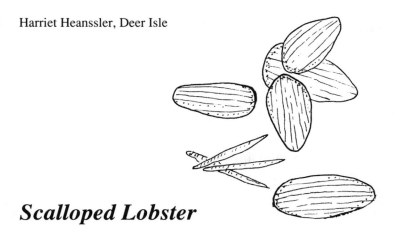

Scalloped Lobster

$1^1/2$ cups cooked lobster meat, cut up
1 cup light cream
1 egg, well beaten
$1/2$ teaspoon prepared mustard
1 tablespoon lemon juice
few drops onion juice
$1/2$ teaspoon salt
pepper, if desired
2 tablespoons butter, melted
1 cup soft bread crumbs

     1. Preheat oven to 350°.
     2. Mix all ingredients except bread crumbs and butter.
     3. Combine crumbs with melted butter.
     4. Put mixture in a greased baking dish and cover with buttered crumbs. Bake 30 minutes.

Pat Poitras, Stonington

Row Like Crazy!
Barney Beal was well known along the Maine coast as a most extraordinary man. Once when he needed herring for lobster bait, he took a dory and rowed from Beals Island to Trafton's Island, which is off Milbridge in the Narraguagus, to get some fish. He had a young boy with him and on the way back to Beals, the dory was awash with the sea. The young man became frightened and began to bail out the dory. Barney looked at him and then said, "You'd better stop bailing and row like crazy because if we don't make it by rowing, we won't make it by bailing."
They got back to Beals Island all right, safely, and with the herring. The distance they had traveled was about forty miles right in the eyes of the ocean.

Charles Beal, Milbridge (1963)
Northeast Archives #62025

Poached Lobster in a Microwave

2 cups cooked lobster meat
1 cup white wine
1 tablespoon butter
2 tablespoons mayonnaise
1 teaspoon Dijon mustard
$^1/_2$ teaspoon horseradish
$^1/_2$ teaspoon curry powder (optional)

    1. Place lobster meat, wine, and butter in a casserole dish. Cover and heat in microwave until hot.
    2. Make a cream sauce from mayonnaise, mustard, horseradish, and curry powder. Serve over hot poached lobster.

Walter "Duke" Pushard, North Edgecomb

Lobster and Rice Bake

1 medium onion, sliced in thin strips
$^1/_2$ green pepper, sliced in thin strips
1 cup sliced mushrooms (fresh or canned)
5 tablespoons butter
1 tablespoon olive oil
2 to 3 cups long-grain white rice, cooked al dente
2 to 3 cups cooked lobster meat
$^1/_2$ cup sherry
salt and pepper to taste
4-ounce jar whole pimentoes, sliced in thin strips

    1. Sauté onion, pepper, and mushrooms (if fresh) in half butter and half olive oil, about one tablespoon of each, until slightly crisp.
    2. Mix rice lightly with vegetables and pimentoes.
    3. Preheat oven to 300°.
    4. Sauté lobster meat in the remaining 4 tablespoons of butter for 5 minutes. Pour sherry over lobster and add salt and pepper to taste. Pour lobster mixture over rice and vegetables in casserole dish. Bake for 15 minutes.

Marie Snow, Yarmouth

Stove Top Lobster and Shrimp with Rice

1 clove garlic, finely minced
olive oil
1 green pepper, sliced
1 onion, sliced
1 fresh tomato, chopped
$1/2$ cup cooked lobster meat, chopped
handful of frozen shrimp
1 cup cooked rice
Tabasco sauce
salt and pepper to taste
1 tablespoon rice wine vinegar

     1. In a wok, sauté garlic in some olive oil. Add green pepper and onion. Cook a few minutes, then add tomato, cooked lobster meat, and a handful of shrimp.
     2. Add rice, Tabasco sauce, salt and pepper to taste. Cook 2 to 3 more minutes, and add rice wine vinegar over all. Serve at once.

Paula Colwell, Deer Isle

Barney Beal Gets His Revenge
It seems that Barney Beal was on one of his trips along the coast in his freighter. He stopped at Rockland and, while standing on the dock, he became involved in an argument whether any man there could lift a 1200-pound anchor which lay on the dock.
Several tried it but no one could move it. Then someone turned to Barney and asked him to try. He declined until a man standing nearby said that he would bet him five dollars that he couldn't lift it. Well, Barney couldn't let a challenge like that go by, so he accepted. He walked over, bent down, and lifted the anchor clear of the dock.
When it came to paying off the bet, the fellow backed out. Barney said, "That's all right." He reached down, raised the anchor again, walked to the edge of the wharf, and dropped it—right through the bottom of the boat belonging to the man who had refused to pay off the bet!

Olive Coffin, Steuben (1963)
Northeast Archives #62031

Lobster-Stuffed Fillets

1/4 cup onion, chopped
3 tablespoons butter
3/4 cup bread, shredded
1 cup cooked lobster meat, very finely chopped
pinch of thyme
salt and pepper to taste
6 flounder fillets
1 can cream of shrimp soup
sherry

     1. Sauté onion in butter. Add bread, lobster meat, thyme, salt, and pepper, and blend together.
     2. Preheat oven to 375°.
     3. Spread mixture on each fillet. Roll up and place seam side down in a pan. Heat soup and, while stirring, add enough sherry to thin. Pour over fillets and bake for 25 minutes.

Phyllis Marsters, Fort Myers, Florida

Spaghetti with Lobster White Sauce

2 teaspoons salt
four 1-pound lobsters
1 bay leaf
2 slices lemon
1 stalk celery and leaves
3 peppercorns
2 sprigs parsley
1 pound raw shrimp, shelled and cleaned

     1. To prepare seafood, fill a large 6-quart pot with water. Add salt and bring to a boil. Add the lobsters and all the remaining ingredients except shrimp. Cook 12 minutes and remove lobsters to cool.
     2. Add the shrimp and simmer until pink, about 4 minutes. Remove shrimp and set aside. Reserve one cup of the broth. Cut lobster meat and shrimp in pieces and set aside.

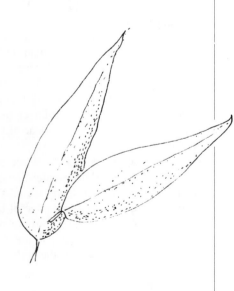

Sauce

6 teaspoons butter
2 teaspoons onion, minced
6 teaspoons flour
1 cup reserved seafood stock
1 cup chicken broth
$1^1/_2$ cups light cream
$^1/_2$ cup dry white wine
$^1/_4$ cup Parmesan cheese, freshly grated
1 teaspoon Dijon mustard
3 to 4 drops of Tabasco sauce
3 teaspoons brandy
1 teaspoon each of salt and white pepper

Spaghetti

1 pound spaghetti or linguine
1 teaspoon salt
3 teaspoons butter
1 teaspoon oil
3 teaspoons Parmesan cheese, grated

1. Melt butter in a pot, add onions, and cook 2 to 3 minutes. Stir in flour, and gradually add the reserved stock, chicken broth, cream, and wine. Cook and stir over low heat until thick and smooth, about 10 minutes.

2. Stir in cheese, mustard, Tabasco sauce, brandy, salt, and pepper. Continue to cook for 10 more minutes. Add lobster meat and shrimp and simmer gently.

3. Cook spaghetti in salted water and drain, and return it to pot. Add butter, oil, and cheese and toss quickly over low heat. Place on a platter and ladle the sauce over it.

Ethyl Teele, Ellsworth

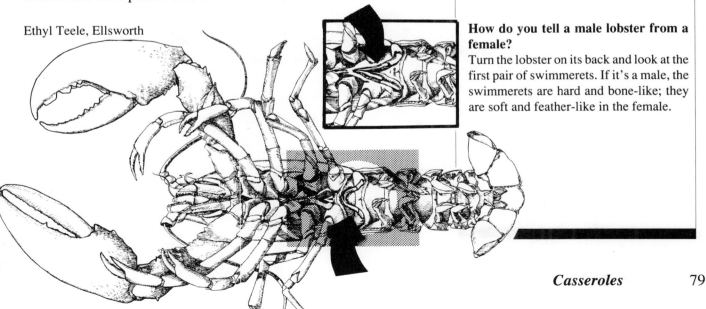

How do you tell a male lobster from a female?
Turn the lobster on its back and look at the first pair of swimmerets. If it's a male, the swimmerets are hard and bone-like; they are soft and feather-like in the female.

Lobster Spaghetti Sauce with Tomatoes

3 lobsters, cooked, and meat cut into small pieces
$^3/_4$ cup olive oil
$^1/_2$ cup onion, chopped
$^1/_2$ green pepper, chopped (optional)
1 can tomato paste
1 large can Italian tomatoes
salt and pepper to taste

    1. Sauté meat in oil to a reddish color. Then add onions and green pepper, and sauté until onions are brown and green pepper is soft. Drain off oil.

    2. Add paste, tomatoes, salt, and pepper to lobster meat and vegetables. Simmer over low heat for a few minutes. Serve over spaghetti.

Linda Kelsey, South Bristol

Seafood Ragout

1 pint fresh oysters, shucked
4 tablespoons butter
4 tablespoons flour
$^3/_4$ cup oyster liquid
$^3/_4$ cup cream
$^3/_4$ teaspoon salt
few grains cayenne pepper
few drops onion juice
$^1/_4$ teaspoon pepper
$^3/_4$ cup cooked lobster meat, diced
$1^1/_2$ teaspoons sauterne or lemon juice
1 tablespoon parsley, finely chopped

1. Cook oysters in their juice, only until they plump up and the edges begin to curl. Drain off the juice and reserve for sauce.

2. Melt the butter and add flour to make a roux.

3. Add oyster liquid, cream, and seasonings and stir slowly over low heat until thickened.

4. Add oysters, lobster meat, wine, and parsley. Serve as is with cooked rice, in a ramekin, or top with cheese and buttered crumbs and bake as a casserole. May also be served with toast points.

Harriet Heanssler, Deer Isle

Rich Stanley banding a lobster

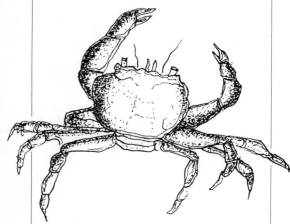

Crabmeat Loaf with Lobster Sauce

1^1/$_2$ cups crabmeat, fresh or canned
3 eggs, separated
1 cup soft bread crumbs
4 tablespoons butter, melted
2 teaspoons lemon juice
1 teaspoon green pepper, minced
1 teaspoon celery salt
^{1}/$_4$ teaspoon salt
^{1}/$_8$ teaspoon pepper

　　1. Preheat oven to 375°. This recipe may be baked in a loaf pan or in custard cups.
　　2. Pick over the crabmeat to remove any bits of shell. Beat egg yolks and add crabmeat.
　　3. Stir in crumbs, butter, and lemon juice. Add green pepper, celery salt, salt, and pepper. Fold in egg whites which have been beaten to stiff peaks.
　　4. Fill buttered custard cups two-thirds full and set in pan of hot water. Bake for 25 minutes. Serve with lobster sauce.

Lobster Sauce
2 tablespoons butter or margarine
2 tablespoons flour
salt and pepper to taste
1 cup milk
^{1}/$_2$ cup cheddar cheese, cubed
^{1}/$_2$ cup cooked lobster meat, cubed

　　1. Prepare a white sauce by melting the butter, adding flour and seasonings, and then slowly stirring in the milk.
　　2. When the sauce is thickened and smooth, add cheese and allow it to melt. Add lobster meat. Spoon lobster sauce over each serving of crabmeat loaf.

Pat Carver, Beals

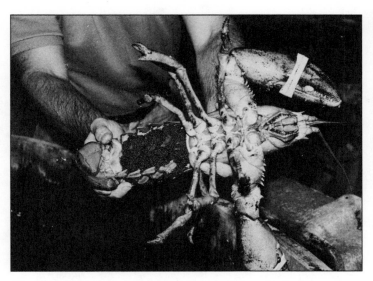
Female lobster with eggs called "berried" females by lobstermen

Edna's Maine Seafood Supreme

2 cups shrimp, cooked and cleaned
1 cup scallops, poached for 5 minutes
1 cup cooked lobster meat
1 cup fresh crabmeat
1$^{1}/_{2}$ sticks butter
9 tablespoons flour
1 teaspoon salt, pepper to taste
2 cups milk
1 cup cream
3 egg yolks, slightly beaten
1 cup Swiss cheese, shredded
1 cup white wine
potato chips, crumbled

    1. Preheat oven to 350°.
    2. Cut larger shellfish into bite-sized pieces.
    3. To make a sauce, melt the butter and stir in flour, salt, and pepper. Heat milk and cream and add slowly to the roux. When the sauce is thickened, add the egg yolks and cook over low heat for 5 minutes.
    4. Add cheese and wine. Then add all the shellfish and pour into a buttered casserole. Cover with crumbled potato chips and bake 15 minutes.

Jane Alley, South Bristol

Jack Merrill and sternman Rich Stanley, 1988

Seafood Casserole

$^1\!/_2$ pound each of fresh haddock, scallops, and shrimp
1 cup cooked lobster meat
1 cup crabmeat
lemon juice
1 stick butter or margarine
1 can cream of shrimp soup
$^1\!/_2$ to 1 cup milk
3 tablespoons white wine or sherry

     1. Poach haddock and scallops in a small amount of water to which a little lemon juice has been added. Drain and set aside.
     2. If you use fresh Maine shrimp, boil a small amount of water (about $^1\!/_2$ cup) with a few drops of lemon juice, add whole shrimp, and cook 2 to 3 minutes. Then clean shrimp. If you clean shrimp first, boil water, add shrimp, bring to a boil again, and simmer for about 45 seconds until they turn opaque.
     3. Sauté crabmeat and lobster meat very lightly.
     4. Make a sauce by mixing soup with melted butter or margarine, and add milk until desired consistency.
     5. Preheat oven to 350°.
     6. Cut haddock, scallops, and lobster meat to desired size and put all seafood in a greased casserole dish. Pour sauce over the seafood and bake for 15 minutes, or until heated thoroughly.

Connie Merrill, Falmouth

Vinalhaven, 1981

Kat's Seafood Bake with Vegetables

1¹/₂ cups cooked lobster meat
1¹/₂ cups crabmeat
1 cup mayonnaise
¹/₂ cup green pepper, chopped
¹/₄ cup onion, minced
1¹/₂ cups celery, finely cut
¹/₂ teaspoon salt
1 teaspoon Worcestershire sauce
2 cups potato chips, crushed
paprika

    1. Preheat oven to 400°.
    2. Combine all ingredients except the potato chips.
    3. Place in a shallow, buttered dish and top with potato chips and paprika. Bake 15 minutes.

Kathy Kane, Surry

Kathy's Scalloped Seafood Casserole

4 tablespoons butter
2 cups fresh scallops
2 cups cooked lobster meat
4 heaping tablespoons flour
2 cups all-purpose cream, warmed
$^1/_2$ teaspoon salt
$^1/_4$ teaspoon pepper
$^1/_4$ teaspoon celery salt
$^1/_2$ teaspoon Worcestershire sauce
8 Ritz crackers, crumbled and softened in butter
paprika

     1. Preheat oven to 425°.
     2. Melt butter in skillet and sauté scallops and lobster meat. Then blend in the flour.
     3. Add cream, salt, pepper, celery salt, and Worcestershire sauce.
     4. Remove from the stove, pour in buttered casserole, and top with cracker crumbs. Sprinkle with paprika and bake for 10 minutes.

Kathy Kane, Surry

Wilder Dolliver, Bass Harbor, 1959

Barney Beal's Last Great Feat
Barney Beal was known far and wide for his strength, and it was his strength that killed him. He often would hook his fingers in the front of a dory and pull it up the beach. He was living on Pond Island, in Milbridge Bay, at the time of his death, and this is what caused it.

He had come in from tending his traps. He got out at the low-water mark, putting the painter of the boat over his shoulder, and started up the beach. As he dragged the dory over the seawall, he broke a blood vessel in his heart and died instantly.

Charles Beal, Milbridge (1963)
Northeast Archives #62030

We have found a growing number of gourmets who love to experiment with lobster. And, even though many think of lobster only as an American food, it has achieved a reputation throughout the world for its excellent flavor, high nutritional value, and versatility in seafood cookery. Many of the recipes included in this chapter have an international flavor. These exotic and savory recipes are sure to impress your guests or your family.

Governor Edmund Muskie with Claramae Turner and Shirley Jones (stars in the film "Carousel") at The Lobster, a restaurant where the first downeast clambake in New York was staged

Chapter 8
Lobster Exotica

Crêpes Filled with Lobster Newburg

1 cup cooked lobster meat, cut into bite-sized cubes
3 tablespoons butter
2 tablespoons shallots, finely chopped
1 tablespoon paprika
1 tablespoon flour
1 cup milk
$^1/_2$ cup heavy cream
salt to taste, if desired
freshly ground black pepper
1 tablespoon Madeira wine
1 egg yolk
pinch of cayenne pepper
8 crêpes

1. Melt 2 tablespoons of the butter in a saucepan and add the shallots and paprika. Cook briefly, stirring. Sprinkle with flour, stirring with a wire whisk.

2. Add the milk, stirring rapidly with the whisk. Add the cream and any liquid that accumulated from cutting up the lobster. Add salt and pepper to taste.

3. Add the Madeira and egg yolk, stirring rapidly with the whisk. Stir in the cayenne pepper.

4. Melt the remaining tablespoon of butter and add the cubed lobster, shaking the skillet and stirring just until the lobster pieces are heated through.

5. Put the cream and egg sauce through a strainer. Pour half of the sauce over the lobster pieces and stir to blend. Use equal, small portions of the sauce with lobster pieces to fill each of 8 crêpes. About 2 tablespoons of filling will suffice for each crêpe. Fold the crêpe over. Spoon the remaining sauce without the lobster meat over the filled crêpes.

Basic Crêpes (makes 5 to 6)
1 egg
$^1/_2$ cup flour
salt, if desired
$^1/_2$ cup plus 2 tablespoons milk
2 tablespoons butter

1. Put the egg, flour, and salt into a mixing bowl and

Buying the Wind
Fishermen used to believe if they wanted some wind, they'd throw a coin in the water. Well, Grover Merchant wanted wind so he threw a nickel in. Instead of asking for a couple of pennies' worth, he asked for a nickel's worth—and he got drowned right out there! A nickel could buy a lot more in those days!

Rollins Kelley, Beals (1990)

Sea Goddess Feature, Department of Sea and Shore Fisheries, 1959

start beating and blending with a wire whisk. Add the milk, stirring.

2. Melt 1 tablespoon of the butter in a 7- or 8-inch pan. When it is melted, pour the butter into the crêpe batter.

3. Line a mixing bowl with a sieve and pour the batter into the sieve. Strain the batter, pushing any solids through with a rubber spatula.

4. Melt the remaining tablespoon of butter and use this to brush the pan each time, or as necessary, before making a crêpe.

5. Brush the pan lightly and place it on the stove. When the pan is hot but not burning, add 2 tablespoons of the batter and swirl it around neatly to completely cover the bottom of the pan. Cook over moderately high heat for 30 to 40 seconds, or until lightly browned on the bottom. Turn the crêpe and cook the second side for about 15 seconds. Turn the crêpe out onto a sheet of waxed paper.

Paula Colwell, Deer Isle

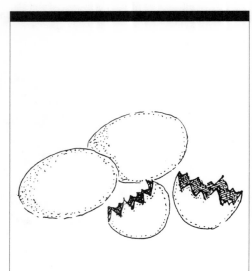

Lobster Crêpes
(makes 12 to 14 crêpes)

3 extra-large eggs
³/₄ cup whole milk
³/₄ cup water
3 tablespoons butter or margarine, melted and cooled
1 cup all-purpose sifted flour
¹/₄ teaspoon salt

1. Beat the eggs well. Add the milk, water, and melted butter.
2. Stir in the flour and salt and beat the whole mixture thoroughly. Cover and let stand overnight in the refrigerator.
3. To cook, heat a crêpe pan or medium-sized frying pan to hot using solid vegetable shortening. Stir crêpe mixture frequently between pouring each one.
4. Pour about ¹/₄ cup of the mixture into the pan, swirl the pan to spread it to 6 inches in diameter, and cook about 1¹/₂ minutes. Turn gently with a spatula, cook about 30 seconds more, and then remove to cooling rack covered with a paper towel. The first crêpe is a test. It should be a "pretty" brown on the first side.
5. When all are cooked, cool them, and use or freeze for later. These can be made in advance and frozen in stacks of three or four, divided by plastic wrap, and put into plastic bags. Separate number to be used and defrost thoroughly. Recipe may be doubled.

Filling (enough for 6 crêpes)
6 tablespoons butter or margarine, melted
1 cup flour
2 cans evaporated milk
1 cup celery, finely diced
1 cup water
1 tablespoon chervil or dill weed
4 cups lobster meat, coarsely diced
³/₄ cup Gruyère (or Swiss) cheese, grated

1. Make a thick cream sauce by melting the butter and adding the flour to make a roux. Then add the milk slowly, using a whisk, and cook over low heat until thickened.

2. Cook the celery in water until soft and add to the cream sauce with the seasoning. Cook a few minutes, remove from heat, and refrigerate until the lobster is added to finish the entrée.

3. Preheat oven to 350˚.

4. Reserve about 6 tablespoons of the sauce. Combine the balance of the sauce with lobster meat. Divide and place a scoop on the lighter side of 6 crêpes, fold crêpes over, and lay them in a greased pan.

5. Top each crêpe with 1 tablespoon of the reserved sauce and about 2 tablespoons grated cheese. Bake about 20 minutes or until cheese is melted and mixture looks ready to bubble out of the crêpes. Serve immediately on heated plates.

Gretchen Stearns, Stonington

Sea Goddess Feature, Department of Sea and Shore Fisheries, 1959

When my father started out in a fishing vessel, if he dropped the hatch cover down the hole, he'd put her right back on the mooring. He wouldn't go fishing that day—it was bad luck.

Rollins Kelley, Beals (1990)

Lobster-Stuffed Chicken Rolls

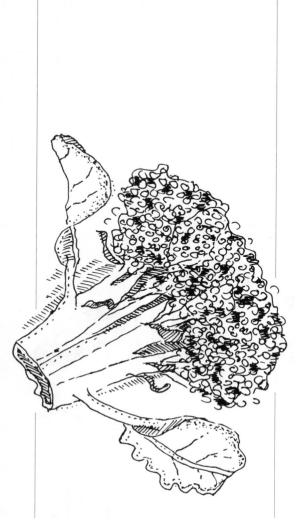

4 boneless chicken breasts, skinned and flattened
$^1/_2$ to 1 cup cooked lobster meat, chopped
$^1/_4$ cup green onions, chopped
1 cup water chestnuts, chopped
$^1/_2$ cup broccoli, chopped
$^1/_2$ cup mushrooms, sliced
Bisquick and small amount of milk (for coating)

    1. Mix lobster meat, green onions, water chestnuts, broccoli, and mushrooms. Place in the middle of a flattened chicken breast and roll. Secure with toothpicks.
    2. Mix Bisquick with a small amount of milk to moisten. Dip each roll in the coating mixture. Fry in oil until just golden brown. Keep warm in a 300° oven. Before serving, make sauce.

Sauce
$^1/_4$ cup peach or apricot preserves
$^1/_2$ cup brown sugar
2 tablespoons apple cider vinegar
2 tablespoons soy sauce
$^1/_2$ teaspoon dry mustard
$^1/_4$ teaspoon garlic powder

    1. Combine all ingredients in a saucepan and cook until smooth.
    2. Serve sauce over warm chicken rolls.

Kathy Brazer, Ogunquit

Paul Venno, Cape Rosier, 1989

When Uncle Charlie was leaving the mooring, if anybody swung his boat away from the sun (counterclockwise), he'd go back and put it on the mooring.

Leta Beal, Beals (1990)

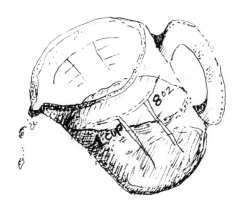

Lobster Diables

4 tablespoons butter
4 tablespoons flour
1 teaspoon dry mustard
1 teaspoon salt
dash of cayenne pepper
2 cups milk
1 teaspoon Worcestershire sauce
$^1/_2$ cup Parmesan cheese, grated
2 tablespoons white wine
1 teaspoon onion or shallots, minced
2 tablespoons butter or margarine
4 cups cooked lobster meat
1 tablespoon parsley, minced
Parmesan cheese, grated (for topping)
pastry shells (optional)

1. Melt 4 tablespoons butter in a saucepan and stir in flour, mustard, salt, and cayenne pepper.

2. Add milk and cook, stirring until thickened. Remove from heat and fold in Worcestershire sauce, grated cheese, and wine.

3. Sauté onion in 2 tablespoons butter until soft. Add lobster meat, parsley, and mustard cream sauce. Spoon into scallop baking shells, individual baking dishes, or baked pastry shells. Sprinkle with Parmesan cheese. Serve at once or brown under broiler.

Pat Poitras, Stonington

One time the old sailor skippers wouldn't start a trip on Friday because it was bad luck. Even today some boat builders won't launch a boat on a Friday.

If anyone mentioned the word "pig" aboard my Uncle Vernal's boat, he wouldn't fish—he was done for the day.

Earlon Beal, Beals (1990)

Italian Lobster

2 tablespoons butter
1 tablespoon onion, diced
1 clove garlic, minced
2 tablespoons green pepper, diced
$1/4$ cup mushrooms, sliced
salt and pepper
1 teaspoon oregano
1 cup tomato sauce
1 cup cooked lobster meat, cut up
Parmesan cheese, grated

    1. Preheat oven to 350°.
    2. Combine all ingredients except the tomato sauce, lobster meat, and Parmesan cheese in a saucepan. Simmer for 5 minutes.
    3. Add tomato sauce and lobster meat.
    4. Pour into a casserole dish and top with Parmesan cheese. Bake for 15 minutes.

Georgie Jackson, Wiscasset

Lobster Linguine with Vegetables

8 tablespoons butter
1 tablespoon olive oil
1 garlic clove, minced
2 small white onions, chopped
1 large carrot, chopped
1 tablespoon parsley, chopped
pinch of crushed red pepper
two 1-pound live lobsters
1 tablespoon salt
freshly ground black pepper
1 pound linguine

    1. Heat butter and oil and sauté the garlic, onions, carrot, parsley, and red pepper until onions are soft.
    2. Cook the lobsters in boiling water with salt in a 10-quart pot. Remove immediately when they turn red, but save the liquid in the pot. When cool, remove the meat from shells

Grandfather believed that if you stuck a knife up in the deck of a boat, you weren't going to get any fish. And you couldn't ring the bell on the boat. If he saw you reach up and grab that string to ring the bell, he'd rave for an hour.

Avery Kelley, Beals (1990)

and dice. Return the shells to the pot and boil the liquid, uncovered, for 40 minutes. Strain the broth and set aside.

3. Add the lobster meat to the vegetables. Stir in 1 cup of the strained lobster broth and add pepper. Simmer for 20 minutes, uncovered.

4. Cook linguine in the strained lobster broth until it is al dente and drain. Place in a large hot bowl. Then pour half of the diced lobster and vegetable sauce over the linguine and toss gently. Serve in hot soup bowls with remaining lobster and vegetable sauce spooned on top.

Daphne Burke, Stonington

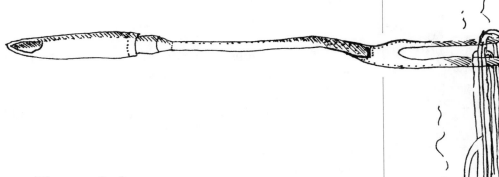

Lobster Fettucini

2 tablespoons butter
4 tablespoons flour
2 cups milk
$^{1}/_{4}$ cup Swiss cheese, grated
$^{1}/_{4}$ cup provolone cheese, grated
3 tablespoons white wine, optional
1 teaspoon garlic, chopped
black pepper
2 tablespoons fresh basil, chopped
1 cup cooked lobster meat, cut up

1. Melt butter in a double boiler and stir in flour to make a roux. Slowly add milk and stir constantly until thickened.

2. Add cheeses, wine, and seasonings, and cook until smooth.

3. Mix in lobster meat. Serve over spinach fettucini or noodles.

Cindy Brown, North Edgecomb

Lobster Fra Diavolo

2 live lobsters, about 1½ pounds each
½ cup olive oil
1 large clove garlic, finely chopped
salt and black pepper
½ small onion, chopped
1 pound fresh tomatoes, peeled and chopped
2 tablespoons tomato paste, dissolved in 2 tablespoons water
⅔ cup white wine
4 teaspoons fresh parsley, chopped
1 teaspoon oregano
½ teaspoon red pepper

     1. Wash lobsters. Chop off claws and cut lobsters into three pieces each. Crack claws with flat side of knife, leaving the shells in place.
     2. Heat oil in a large skillet until very hot. Add lobsters and cook over high heat for 3 to 4 minutes. Add garlic. Then with 1-minute intervals of cooking between them, add salt, black pepper, and onion.
     3. When lobsters are red, add tomatoes and paste.
     4. After 2 to 3 minutes, add wine, parsley, oregano, and red pepper. Stir. The fire should be hot, and the whole cooking process should not take more than 15 minutes. Serve over your favorite pasta.

Gregory Griffin, Cape Elizabeth

Lobster Mexicana

2 cups cooked lobster meat
2 tomatoes, chopped
¼ cup green pepper, chopped
½ teaspoon ground cumin
¼ teaspoon ground allspice
⅛ teaspoon ground red pepper
½ cup all-purpose cream
2 cups unsalted cracker crumbs
⅓ cup margarine or butter, melted
limes, cut into wedges or slices, and nachos, for garnishes

In Bass Harbor there was a superstition against Gott's Island Blue. You couldn't have clothes, an engine, or anything around the boat that color blue.

Willard was the oldest sternman I ever had. He would never take up a hatch cover and lay it upside down—it was a bad omen.

Richard Black, Bass Harbor (1990)

1. Preheat oven to 375°.

2. Mix lobster meat, tomatoes, and green pepper. Arrange in an oblong 11x7-inch dish.

3. Blend spices and cream. Pour ¼ cup of spiced cream over lobster mixture.

4. Mix crumbs and melted butter or margarine. Sprinkle over lobster combination. Pour remaining cream over crumbs. Cook uncovered for 30 minutes. Garnish with limes and nachos. Serve with rice and salad.

Nova Scotia Department of Fisheries, Halifax, N.S.

Lobster with Chinese Vegetables

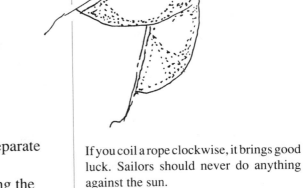

3 cups cooked lobster meat
1 package frozen Chinese pea pods
3 medium stalks bok choy
2 tablespoons vegetable oil
2 cloves garlic, finely chopped
2 thin slices ginger root, crushed
8½-ounce can water chestnuts, drained and thinly sliced
8½-ounce can bamboo shoots, drained
½ cup mushrooms, sliced
¾ cup chicken broth
2 tablespoons cornstarch
2 tablespoons soy sauce
1 teaspoon salt
1 teaspoon sugar
¼ teaspoon white pepper
2 green onions, thinly sliced
hot cooked rice

1. Cut lobster meat into 1-inch pieces.

2. Rinse pea pods under running cold water to separate and then drain.

3. Separate leaves from bok choy stems, reserving the leaves. Cut stems into ¼-inch slices.

4. Heat oil in wok until hot. Cook and stir garlic and ginger root over medium heat until brown. Add pea pods, bok choy stems, water chestnuts, bamboo shoots, and mushrooms. Cook and stir over medium heat for 2 minutes.

5. Stir in one-half the chicken broth and reduce heat. Cover and simmer for 1 minute.

If you coil a rope clockwise, it brings good luck. Sailors should never do anything against the sun.

It's bad luck to change a boat's name.

Never whistle on board because it will cause the wind to come up.

Anonymous

6. Mix the remaining chicken broth, the cornstarch, soy sauce, salt, sugar, and white pepper. Stir into vegetable mixture. Cook and stir until thickened, about 30 seconds.

7. Tear bok choy leaves into bite-sized pieces. Add leaves and lobster meat to vegetable mixture and heat until hot. Garnish with green onions and serve with rice.

Paula Colwell, Deer Isle

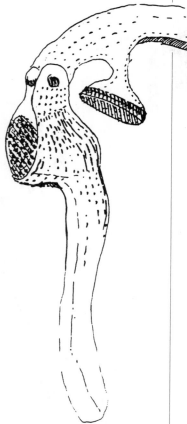

Lobster Curry

2 tablespoons butter
$^3/_4$ cup onions, chopped
$^1/_2$ cup celery, chopped
$^1/_2$ cup apples, chopped
$^1/_2$ cup carrots, grated
1 clove garlic, crushed
1 tablespoon curry powder
1 tablespoon flour
$^1/_4$ teaspoon ginger
$1^1/_4$ cups chicken stock
$^1/_4$ cup all-purpose cream
2 cups cooked lobster meat
salt and pepper to taste

1. Melt butter in a large saucepan and sauté onions, celery, apples, carrots, and garlic until tender.

2. Add curry powder, flour, ginger, and chicken stock. Simmer for 20 minutes. Put this mixture in a food processor and blend until smooth. Return to saucepan.

3. Add cream, lobster meat, salt, and pepper. Simmer for 5 minutes, until heated through. Serve with rice.

Serves 4.

Jean Aldrich, Hancock

Ghost Ships Ahoy!
There's a ghost ship out near John's Island. It always appears out of the fog. Some say it's the ghost of a pirate ship that sank. Ohers say that Captain Kidd buried treasure on John's Island and anytime anyone gets near the treasure, the fog shuts in and a ghost ship comes out of the fog. Many of the men on Swan's Island claim they've seen it.

Anna Carlson, Swan's Island (1967)
Northeast Archives #30253

Lobster with Thai Coconut Curry Sauce

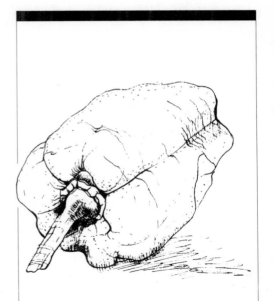

four 1¼-pound live lobsters
1½ tablespoons peanut oil
2 cloves garlic, minced
*3 teaspoons red Thai curry paste
1 sweet red pepper, cut into ¼ inch strips
1 sweet yellow pepper, cut into ¼ inch strips
1 can *unsweetened* coconut milk
¾ cup heavy cream
2 small tomatoes, each cut into 8 wedges
4 scallions, cut into 2-inch lengths (include the green tops)
½ cup fresh basil leaves, packed
*½ teaspoon Nam Pla (also called Thai fish sauce)

1. In a large pot, bring 2 inches of cold water to a boil. Add lobsters and cover. As soon as water returns to a boil, steam lobsters for 9 minutes. Remove lobsters from pot and cool.

2. Lightly crack claws and knuckles. Remove all meat from claws, knuckles, and tails. Slice tail meat in half lengthwise. Remove tomalley from body cavity and set aside.

3. Heat the oil in a large sauté pan. Add garlic and curry and cook over medium heat for 1 minute, or until garlic is golden. Add red and yellow peppers and sauté for 2 minutes.

4. Add coconut milk and reduce by half over high heat. Add cream and simmer for 3 to 4 minutes until slightly thickened.

5. Add tomatoes, scallions, basil, Nam Pla, and lobster meat. Continue cooking for 1 minute, or until heated thoroughly. Stir in the tomalley. Serve with rice.

Serves 4.

* Available at Asian markets

Cheryl Lewis, Cafe Always, Portland

Lobster Stir-Fry

2 tablespoons oil
1 pound cooked lobster meat, cut up
1 large onion, sliced
$1^1/_2$ large green peppers, cut in rings
1 cup celery, sliced
1 clove garlic, minced
$^3/_4$ cup chicken broth
2 tablespoons cornstarch
3 tablespoons soy sauce
$^1/_2$ teaspoon pepper
2 large tomatoes, chopped
4 cups cooked rice

1. Heat oil in a skillet, add lobster meat, and cook 2 minutes.
2. Add onion, green peppers, celery, and garlic. Cover and steam 2 minutes.
3. Dissolve the cornstarch in the chicken broth mixed with soy sauce and pepper. Stir in lobster mixture.
4. Add the tomatoes. Cook, stirring 2 minutes or until sauce is clear and thickened. Serve over beds of fluffy rice.

Harriet Heanssler, Deer Isle

How big do lobsters grow?
The largest known lobster caught in Maine measured 36 inches from the rostrum (back) to the end of the tail. One of the largest known ever caught is a 42-pound, seven-ounce monster on display (dead and mounted) at the Museum of Science in Boston.

Governor John H. Reed serves lobster to Mr. and Mrs. Mike Douglas

Lynn Carver Alley and Walter Carver, Beals, 1958

Lobster from the Orient

2 tablespoons oil
2 cups cooked lobster meat, cut into pieces
1 small clove garlic, minced
2 tablespoons rum
$^1/_2$ cup chicken broth
1 cup bean sprouts
1 cup water chestnuts, sliced
1 cup fresh broccoli, cut into pieces
1$^1/_2$ cups Chinese cabbage, coarsely cut
salt and pepper
1 egg, beaten

   1. Heat the oil in a skillet and add lobster meat and garlic. Cook briefly and then add the rum, broth, and vegetables. Simmer uncovered for 5 minutes. Season with salt and pepper.
   2. Add a little of the sauce from the skillet to the lightly beaten egg. Stir the egg mixture into the remainder of the lobster sauce. *Do not let it boil.* Serve with rice.

Nova Scotia Department of Fisheries, Halifax, N.S.

Lobsters the Size of Children!

During the early 1930s, a large, metal span bridge was constructed, connecting the mainland with Verona Island, an island off the shore of Bucksport, Maine. Several deep-sea divers were employed to aid the construction workers in fortifying the base supports beneath the water's surface.

One day three divers quickly came to the surface and said they were all through. The other two divers did not come to the surface. One of the three lucky divers claimed that he actually saw several lobsters the size of small children. Unfortunately, two of the divers did not notice the giant lobsters until it was too late!

Charles H. McIntosh, Jr., Rockland (1966)
Northeast Archives #27418

Pan-Fried Lobster with Pork

one 2-pound lobster, killed but not boiled
4 ounces fresh pork
4 tablespoons peanut oil
2 garlic cloves, minced
1 egg, beaten
2 teaspoons ginger, minced
1 tablespoon white wine
2 scallions, white part only, cut into fine slices

Lobster Marinade
$1^1/_2$ teaspoons light soy sauce
1 tablespoon oyster sauce
$^3/_4$ teaspoon salt
1 teaspoon sugar
pinch of white pepper
2 teaspoons sesame oil

Pork Marinade
$^1/_8$ teaspoon salt
$^1/_4$ teaspoon light soy sauce
$^1/_4$ teaspoon sesame oil
$^1/_2$ teaspoon cornstarch
$^1/_2$ teaspoon sugar

1. Combine all ingredients for lobster marinade in a bowl and mix well. Cut lobster into bite-sized pieces and place in lobster marinade for 30 minutes. Reserve.

2. Combine all ingredients for pork marinade in a bowl and mix well. Dice pork into $^1/_4$-inch pieces. Place in pork marinade for 20 minutes. Reserve.

3. Heat a wok over high heat for 1 minute. Add 1 tablespoon of the peanut oil and coat wok. Add 1 minced garlic clove. When it browns, add pork mixture, separating pieces of pork. Let cook for 3 minutes. Turn over and mix thoroughly.

4. When pork turns white, add beaten egg, and mix into a soft scramble. Remove from wok and reserve. Wash and dry wok.

5. Drain lobster and reserve marinade.

6. Heat the wok over high heat for 1 minute. Add 3 tablespoons peanut oil and coat wok. Add the minced ginger

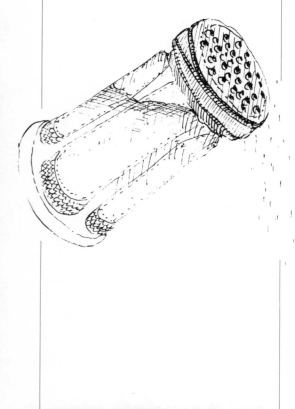

and stir. Add second minced garlic clove. When garlic browns, add lobster pieces.

7. Spread lobster pieces in a single layer, turning wok side to side to spread heat evenly. Turn over pieces. Add wine at edges of wok and allow it to run down. Mix thoroughly.

8. When lobster meat reddens, add pork-egg mixture. Mix all ingredients thoroughly. If too dry, add a little of the reserved lobster marinade. Add scallions and mix thoroughly. Heat and serve.

Paula Colwell, Deer Isle

Richard Black, Bass Harbor, 1959

My Island Ghost

When I was stationed on Nash's Light, a one-man lighthouse, one night at sunset while waiting for the light to burn up, I happened to look around the island from the windows of the tower and I noticed a woman's face in one of the tower windows. I moved about for I knew it must be a shadow. It wasn't a shadow. I could make out a woman's face. She looked old-fashioned with her hair parted in the middle and laid down close to her forehead. But her low-necked dress was something out of the ordinary. I looked at the light in the tower to check it and she disappeared. I was afraid to go by myself for fear I would see her or meet her. Being timid of ghosts, I kind of expected to see her.

Later, my grandson came out during his vacation and we set a few lobster traps. He wanted this day to move them into the kelp by the shore so I told him to go ahead and I would stay on shore and watch him. He took the pod and rowed around the shore and brought the lobster pots in shore. I was standing up leaning against a telephone pole watching him when something brushed by me. I looked and there stood that old lady. She never spoke and neither did I. I told my wife about it. I lost thirty pounds in the time between her two visits to me. We moved from Nash's Island Lighthouse.

Captain Harry Dobbin, Jonesport (1963)
Northeast Archives #15274

Savory American Lobster

two 1¹/₂ pound live lobsters
¹/₃ cup olive oil
3 tablespoons butter or margarine
1 small onion, minced
1 garlic clove, minced
6 medium tomatoes, peeled and chopped
1 cup dry white wine
¹/₄ cup brandy
3 tablespoons tomato paste
1¹/₂ teaspoons salt
1 teaspoon dried thyme
parsley sprigs, for garnish

     1. Place the lobster on its back and insert the point of a knife through the back shell where the tail and body meet, to sever the vein. (For complete instructions on how to split a live lobster, please refer to Chapter 1, "Basics: How to Start.")
     2. With a knife, cut the lobster in half lengthwise through the shell. Remove the dark vein from the tail. Leave the greenish-gray tomalley and roe, if present.
     3. Remove the sand sac from the head. Break off the claws and cut each claw across joints into 3 pieces. Crack claws and cut lobster into chunks.
     4. Heat oil in an 8-quart dutch oven over high heat. Cook lobster pieces until shell turns red, about 5 minutes. Remove pieces and set aside.
     5. Melt butter in the dutch oven. Add onion and garlic and cook until tender, stirring occasionally. Add the remaining ingredients (except the parsley) and heat to boiling.
     6. Reduce heat, cover, and simmer for 20 minutes, stirring occasionally. Add lobster pieces, cover, and heat through. Garnish with parsley sprigs.

Pat Carver, Beals

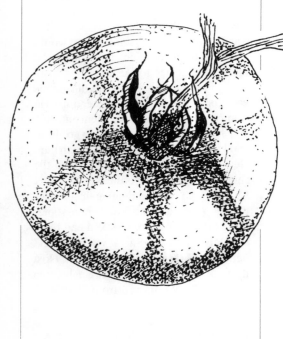

Lobster Creole

2 tablespoons butter
1¹/₂ cups onion, chopped
1 cup celery, finely chopped
1 cup green pepper, finely chopped
2 cloves garlic, minced
1 teaspoon fresh parsley, snipped into pieces
15-ounce can tomato sauce
1 cup water
1 teaspoon salt
¹/₈ teaspoon red pepper
2 bay leaves, crushed
1 pound cooked lobster meat, sautéed in a little butter
3 cups cooked rice

    1. Melt butter in a saucepan and sauté onion, celery, green pepper, and garlic until tender.
    2. Remove from heat and stir in tomato sauce, water, and seasonings. Simmer 10 minutes. Stir in lobster meat and heat over medium heat 10 to 20 minutes. Serve over rice.

Kathy Kane, Surry

Twice-Baked Potatoes with Lobster

4 large baking potatoes
salt and freshly ground black pepper to taste
4 tablespoons sweet butter
¹/₃ cup onion, finely chopped
¹/₂ cup fresh mushrooms, finely chopped
2 cups cooked lobster meat
1 cup dry white vermouth
¹/₂ cup crème fraîche (recipe follows)
¹/₂ cup Jarlsberg cheese, grated, plus additional cheese for potato topping
1 to 2 tablespoons heavy cream (optional)

    1. Preheat oven to 375°.
    2. Scrub and dry the potatoes. Cut a small deep slit in

Haunted Island
Mark Island was said to have buried treasure on it which the pirates buried there. The pirates left two men to guard it. They did this until their death. It is said that the spirits of the men are still guarding it. And if anyone attempts to go on Mark Island, their boats will spring a leak. If they succeed in making it ashore, the Island will be surrounded with a terrific storm around its haunted shores.

Maurice Alley, Jonesport (1963)
Northeast Archives #15281

the top of each. Set potatoes on the middle rack of oven and bake for about 1 hour, or until tender.

3. Let potatoes cool slightly, cut off and discard the tops, and scrape the potato pulp into a bowl, being careful not to scrape so deeply that you tear the potato skins. Salt and pepper the potato shells and reserve them. Mash the potato pulp and set aside.

4. Melt the butter in a small skillet and sauté the chopped onion, covered, until tender and lightly colored, about 25 minutes.

5. Add the mushrooms and sauté for another 5 minutes. Stir in the lobster. Season with salt and pepper, add the vermouth, then raise heat to a boil. Stir frequently over high heat until all liquid has boiled away. Stir in crème fraîche (recipe follows) and remove from heat.

6. Combine lobster mixture with the reserved mashed potato pulp and $1/2$ cup Jarlsberg cheese. Taste, correct seasoning, and add heavy cream if the mixture seems too dry.

7. Increase oven heat to 400°. Stuff the mixture into the reserved potato skins, mounding the fillings slightly. Sprinkle additional grated cheese on top and place on baking sheet. Bake until potatoes are hot and cheese is bubbling.

Crème Fraîche
1 cup heavy cream
1 cup dairy sour cream

1. Whisk heavy cream and sour cream together in a bowl. Cover loosely with plastic wrap and let stand in a reasonably warm spot overnight, or until thickened.

2. Cover and refrigerate for at least 4 hours, after which the crème fraîche will be quite thick. The tart flavor will continue to develop as it sits. Makes 2 cups.

Paula Colwell, Deer Isle

How to Hypnotize a Lobster
You must start with a real lively one. Holding the lobster by the body in your left hand, start stroking (with your right hand) the lobster's tail in a downward motion, curling the tail as you go. Do this until the lobster is inert.
Moving carefully, you may stand the lobster on its head, using claws for support. He will stand like this until you wake him up.
To awaken the lobster, take it by the body and shake it.

Pat Carver, Beals (1989)

l eftover is really a misnomer here. If you talk to anyone who loves lobster, it is never considered to be a leftover! However, we wanted to have a chapter that would include all the recipes that work well with small pieces of lobster meat picked from the body after the claws and tail have been eaten.

From newburgs, omelets, and hash, to cutlets and lobster cakes, all recipes can be made with any amount of lobster meat you might have on hand. However, if you have large claw or tail meat, it is better to cut it into small pieces or chop it before beginning. At any rate, no one will ever guess that you're serving them leftovers!

Gilbert's, Pemaquid, 1949

Chapter 9

LUSCIOUS LOBSTER:

The Leftover Way

Lobster Newburg

5 tablespoons butter
2 cups cooked lobster meat, cut up
2 tablespoons sherry
1 tablespoon flour
1 cup all-purpose cream
2 egg yolks, beaten
1 teaspoon lemon juice
salt and paprika to taste

1. In a skillet, melt 3 tablespoons of the butter and heat thoroughly the lobster meat and sherry, being careful not to brown the butter.

2. In another pan, melt the remainder of the butter and blend in the flour.

3. Add cream and stir constantly until the sauce boils and thickens.

4. Remove from heat and add egg yolks, lemon juice, and seasonings. Stir well, add lobster, and stir again. Serve on toast points or egg noodles.

Sharon Blackmore, Deer Isle

Mail-Order Woman
Catalogs were popular back then and Uncle Eben would go through them and he'd see a pretty woman and he thought he could get her. So, he'd call and say, "I want this one right here" and he'd get the money and send it in. And when the dress came, he'd say, "I don't want the dress, I want the woman!" He was some disappointed.

Avery Kelley, Beals (1990)

Weighing lobsters at Bay Point

What happens to old lobster shells?
They are either left behind or lobsters eat them.

No Sherry Lobster Newburg

1 cup evaporated milk
1¹/₂ cups whole milk
¹/₂ can tomato soup
1 tablespoon butter
¹/₂ cup cheese, grated
salt and pepper
2 teaspoons cornstarch, mixed with 1 tablespoon water
dash Worcestershire sauce
4 cups cooked lobster meat, cut into small pieces
2 tablespoons butter
paprika

     1. To make sauce, mix all ingredients *except* the lobster meat, 2 tablespoons butter, and paprika. Cook to thicken.
     2. Sauté the lobster meat slightly in butter and add to the sauce. Sprinkle with paprika. Serve over toast, rice, or noodles.

Kathy Kane, Surry

Seafood Newburg

6 tablespoons butter or margarine
3 tablespoons all-purpose flour
1 teaspoon salt
$^1/_8$ teaspoon nutmeg
3 egg yolks
2 cups half and half
1 cup milk
1 pound cooked, shelled, and deveined shrimp
2 cups cooked lobster meat, cut into small pieces
3 tablespoons sherry (optional)
3 cups hot cooked rice

     1. Melt butter or margarine in a 12-inch skillet over medium-high heat. Stir in flour, salt, and nutmeg until blended.
     2. In a medium bowl, beat egg yolks slightly with a fork and stir in half and half and milk.
     3. Add this to the flour mixture and cook, stirring constantly, until thickened.
     4. Add shrimp, lobster meat, and sherry. Cook over low heat until thoroughly warmed. Serve with hot rice.

Pat Carver, Beals

Seafood Newburg with Mushrooms

1 cup cooked lobster meat, cut into small pieces
1 small 6-ounce can crabmeat or 6 ounces fresh crabmeat
1 small can (4$^1/_4$ ounces) shrimp or $^1/_2$ pound fresh shrimp, shelled and deveined
4 tablespoons butter
2 cans cream of mushroom soup
1 3-ounce can mushrooms or $^1/_4$ pound fresh mushrooms, sliced
1 cup whole milk
$^1/_2$ teaspoon paprika
$^1/_4$ teaspoon nutmeg
$^1/_4$ cup sherry or white wine

     1. Sauté lobster, crabmeat, and shrimp in butter.
     2. Add soup, mushrooms with liquid, milk, and

seasonings. Heat to boiling and simmer 10 minutes. Add wine just before serving.

3. Serve on patty shells or toast with crusts removed.

Susan Smith, Kittery Point

David Dow, Executive Director of the Lobster Institute, 1989

Seafood with Vegetables in Puff Pastry

Frozen puff pastry shells
$1/2$ cup celery, sliced
$1/3$ cup green pepper, cut into strips
2 tablespoons butter
2 tablespoons flour
$1^1/2$ cups milk
1 cup cheddar cheese, shredded
1 teaspoon dry mustard
$1/4$ teaspoon paprika
1 cup cooked, chopped lobster meat, shrimp, and crabmeat
2 tablespoons parsley, chopped

1. Prepare shells as the package directs.

2. Cook celery and pepper in butter until tender. Add flour and cook until smooth and bubbling.

3. Gradually blend in milk, stirring until thickened and smooth.

4. Add remaining ingredients and heat, stirring constantly, until cheese is melted and seafood is hot. Spoon into heated shells.

From recipe book *Fisherman's Fair*, Bailey Island Fire Dept. Auxiliary

How to Make Cull Stew and Other Secrets

To try to convince tourists to buy "culls" (one-clawed lobsters), I used to tell them that culls are always sweeter. Because the lobster only has one claw, all the sweetness is concentrated in the other claw and the tail. (**Editor's note**: Sometimes culls are less expensive because many people don't know this secret!)

To make "cull stew," you go out and get as many culls as you possibly can. Then you cook them all up and eat them—any way you want.

David Dow (Executive Director of the Lobster Institute), Ellsworth, 1990

Lobster Rarebit

1 stick butter
4 to 6 tablespoons flour
2 cups milk
1 cup cheddar cheese, broken into pieces
2 cups cooked lobster meat, cut into small pieces
salt and pepper to taste

1. Make a white sauce by melting the butter, adding the flour to make a roux, and stirring in the milk slowly. Cook over low heat until thickened.
2. Add cheese and stir until melted and smooth.
3. Add lobster meat pieces and heat thoroughly. Season to taste. Serve immediately on toast or crackers.

Donna Vachon, Stetson

Lobster Cakes

2 slices bread without crust
1 to 2 tablespoons milk
2 cups cooked lobster meat, cut into small pieces
$1/4$ teaspoon sage
$1/2$ teaspoon salt
1 tablespoon mayonnaise
1 tablespoon Worcestershire sauce
1 teaspoon parsley, chopped
1 tablespoon baking powder
1 egg, beaten

1. Break bread into pieces and moisten with milk.
2. Add lobster meat and mix with remaining ingredients.
3. Shape into cakes and fry until brown on both sides.

Louise Alley, South Bristol

Too Much of a Hurry!
Uncle Eben was always on the go—walking here and there. One time someone stopped to pick him up and he said, "Oh, I'm in too much of a hurry, dear. Don't have time for a ride!" So they drove right off and left him.

Avery Kelley, Beals (1990)

Lobster à la King in Toast Tulips

1 tablespoon green pepper, chopped
1 tablespoon butter
1 can cream of mushroom soup
$\frac{1}{2}$ cup milk
1 cup cooked lobster meat, diced
2 tablespoons celery, chopped
2 egg yolks
12 slices bread, crusts removed
paprika

1. Sauté green pepper in butter until soft.
2. Mix in soup, add milk, and put in a double boiler.
3. Add lobster, celery, and eggs. Preheat oven to 375°.
4. Press bread slices into muffin pan. Bake for 12 minutes.
5. Pour lobster mixture over toast tulips and garnish with paprika.

Mary Faulkingham, Wiscasset

Lobster Scampi

5 ounces cooked lobster meat, chopped
2 tablespoons butter
1 teaspoon garlic, minced
2 tablespoons olive oil
2 tablespoons white wine
parsley, salt, and pepper

1. Sauté lobster meat in melted butter.
2. Add garlic, olive oil, wine, parsley, salt, and pepper. Heat thoroughly. Serve over rice pilaf.

Barry Johnston, Fisherman's Wharf, Boothbay Harbor

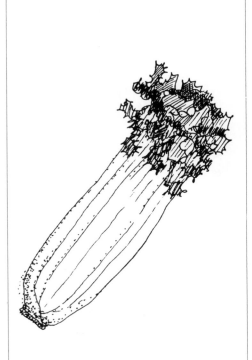

Are lobsters right-handed, left-handed or both?
You can tell whether a lobster is right or left-handed by which side the large crusher claw is on. Lobsters are usually right-handed—the crusher claw is on the right and the smaller pincer or ripper claw is on the left. It is very rare for a lobster to have two crusher claws.

Lobster Omelet

4 eggs
4 tablespoons milk
salt and pepper to taste
2 tablespoons butter
1/2 cup cooked lobster meat, cut into small pieces and warmed in butter

　　　1. Beat eggs until light and fluffy. Add milk, salt, and pepper.
　　　2. Heat butter in an omelet pan and add egg mixture. Cook slowly over low heat.
　　　3. When underside is set, lift omelet slightly with spatula and let uncooked portion flow underneath cooked part.
　　　4. When mixture is almost set, spread warmed lobster meat on top and fold. Cook a few minutes longer.

Paula Colwell, Deer Isle

Lobster Hash

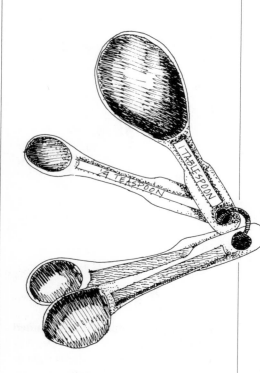

1/4 pound salt pork, chopped
5 large potatoes
cooked meat from three lobsters, cut into small pieces
tomalley
1 teaspoon vinegar
pepper to taste

　　　1. Fry salt pork in frying pan. Pour off one-half amount of grease.
　　　2. Cook 5 potatoes and dice in large pieces.
　　　3. Put lobster meat in frying pan with cooked salt pork and grease, potatoes, tomalley, vinegar, and pepper. Fry all together until it looks red.

Louise Alley, South Bristol

Lobster Farci

1 tablespoon butter
1 tablespoon flour
1 cup milk
little sherry
2 hard-boiled eggs, finely diced
$1/2$ tablespoon fresh parsley, chopped
$1/2$ teaspoon salt
$1/2$ teaspoon pepper
dash nutmeg
2 cups cooked lobster meat, chopped
bread crumbs, mixed with melted butter

1. Preheat oven to 350°.
2. Make a white sauce by melting the butter, adding the flour, and slowly stirring in the milk over low heat until the sauce is thickened.
3. Add the sauce, sherry, eggs, parsley, and seasonings to the lobster in a mixing bowl. Combine all ingredients.
4. Place mixture in a baking dish and cover with buttered crumbs. Bake for about 30 minutes or until crumbs are browned.

Linda Kelsey, South Bristol

Lobsters being shipped from Rockland (from *Deep Waters* magazine)

Just About Frozen
One night Uncle Eben was walking in a snowstorm and he knew there was a farmhouse up ahead of people he knew. He figured if he could just make it to there, he'd get a night to stay because it was blowing a gale, and cold. When he got there, the farmers had gone to bed early. So, he taps on the door and he taps lightly because he doesn't want to wake them up. But, here it's snowing and that's exactly what he wants to do!
The next morning, the farmer hears this tap, tap, tap and he goes to the door and there's Uncle Eben. He's got exposure, hypothermia, and he's right blue and there're icicles hanging off him. The farmer said, "Is that you, Uncle Eben?" And he said, "I am just about frozen. I tapped all night but just as lightly as I could because I didn't want to wake you up."

Avery Kelley, Beals (1990)

After looking through the whole cookbook, Dave Dow, Executive Director of the Lobster Institute, said, "How can you have a lobster cookbook without a recipe for lobster pie?" So, here it is.

Lobster Pie
1 pound lobster meat, cut into pieces
4 cups Ritz crackers, crushed
1 stick butter, melted
$1/2$ cup sherry
$1/2$ pint all-purpose cream

Mix all ingredients together and place in a casserole dish. Cover and bake at 350° for 20 minutes. Uncover and bake 15 more minutes.

Seafood Soufflé

3 tablespoons butter
3 tablespoons flour
1 cup milk
$1/2$ teaspoon salt
$1/8$ teaspoon white pepper
a pinch of nutmeg
sprinkle of cayenne pepper
4 egg yolks
6 egg whites, at room temperature
salt
$3/4$ cup cooked lobster meat, chopped, and/or crabmeat and finely flaked cooked fish (or a mixture of these)
5 tablespoons Swiss cheese, finely grated

1. Melt butter in heavy saucepan over medium heat. Blend in flour, then stir in milk, salt, pepper, nutmeg, and cayenne pepper. Cook, stirring continuously, until sauce thickens slightly.

2. Remove pan from heat. Beat in egg yolks, one at a time, until all have been added. Set mixture aside to cool. Preheat oven to 400°.

3. Beat egg whites with a pinch of salt until they are stiff but not dry. Gently fold 1 cup of these into the cooled white sauce to lighten it. Fold in remaining egg whites and seafood with an up-and-over motion.

4. Butter a soufflé or other deep baking dish, put 3 tablespoons of the cheese in the dish and roll it around until all inner surfaces are covered.

5. Turn the egg mixture into the baking dish and bake 3 minutes at 400°. Then lower the temperature to 375° and bake 35 minutes. Quickly sprinkle the remaining cheese over the soufflé and bake 5 to 10 minutes more, or until set and nicely browned. Serve immediately.

Linda Kelsey, South Bristol

George Partridge, Hancock, 1943

Batter-Fried Lobster

Batter:
$^1/_2$ cup flour
$^1/_4$ teaspoon salt
$^1/_2$ teaspoon paprika
$^1/_4$ teaspoon curry powder
$^1/_4$ teaspoon baking powder
1 egg
$1^1/_2$ teaspoons lemon juice
$^1/_3$ cup milk
2 cups cooked lobster meat from tails and claws, cut into good-sized pieces

    1. Mix together the flour, salt, paprika, curry powder, and baking powder.
    2. Beat the egg and then add the lemon juice and milk.
    3. Beat the liquids into the flour until smooth using a whisk or electric beater. Add a little more milk if batter is too heavy.
    4. Dip pieces of cooked lobster meat into the batter and drop gently into hot fat in a deep fryer. Fry only until golden brown.

Mary Blackmore, Stonington

Electricity Comes to Jonesport (1923)
The night they turned the lights on in Jonesport, Uncle Eben was rowing down from Milbridge in a pod. When he came through Tibbett Narrows, he saw lights and he'd never seen anything like that before. So he got worried. The First World War was on and he thought the Germans had taken over. So he hauled the pod up on Hardwood Island and stayed the night. The next morning he got out from under the pod and took a look and everything looked pretty normal. He rowed down and found out what had happened.

Avery Kelley, Beals (1990)

Editor's note: After much research, we found out that electricity came to Jonesport in 1923. The next day, we received a post card that stated that lights were turned on in Jonesport in November, 1926, in a pouring rain storm.

Lobster Cutlets

1 tablespoon lemon juice
1 cup cooked lobster body meat, cut up into small pieces
1 tablespoon butter
2 tablespoons flour
$1/2$ cup milk
2 egg yolks
paprika, onion seasoning, salt and pepper to taste
1 whole egg, beaten, and mixed with 1 tablespoon water
cracker crumbs
$1/2$ cup bread crumbs (optional)

    1. Pour lemon juice over lobster meat and let stand.

    2. While lobster is marinating, make a thick cream sauce. Melt butter, add flour to make a roux, and whisk in milk, egg yolks, and seasonings. Cook until thick.

    3. Add cream sauce to lobster meat. Cool and shape into patties.

    4. Dip patties in egg and water mixture, roll in cracker crumbs, and fry in hot oil, about 350°, until brown. Drain on paper towel and serve with tartar sauce. (See recipe on page19)

Note: For a simpler version of this recipe, you may add bread crumbs after mixing the cream sauce with the lobster meat, and immediately drop by tablespoonfuls into the hot oil.

Cindy Brown, North Edgecomb

Missy and Jad Dow, 1980

Business As Usual

Uncle Eben was always trying to do business but he wasn't much of a businessman. One of the businesses he went into was candy. Every kid likes candy, so he bought a lot. But, what he'd do is he'd sell it for half price. He got all the candy business. Well, he'd say, "I'm doing big business!" The next thing you'd know, his capital would run out and he couldn't imagine where his money was since he'd sold so much!

Avery Kelley, Beals (1990)

We just couldn't put together a cookbook that expresses the true flavor of Maine without including some of our favorite dessert recipes. We have chosen only those which use fruits and berries native to the state and those, like grapenut pudding and homemade ice cream, which have been served by our grandmothers and great-grandmothers.

Most of the recipes are light enough so they can be served after a full-course meal, and your guests will not feel like they are overindulging. We feel they are a perfect accompaniment to a lobster dinner and a delicious way to end the feast.

Chapter 10

AFTER THE FEAST:

Desserts

Fresh Strawberry Pie

1 quart strawberries
1 cup sugar
3 tablespoons cornstarch
1 cup water
few drops red food coloring (optional)
baked 9-inch pastry shell (recipe follows)

     1. Hull and wash strawberries. Crush about 8 of the largest ones.

     2. Combine sugar and cornstarch in a small saucepan. Add water and the crushed berries. Cook until thick and clear. Add food coloring.

     3. Pour hot mixture over whole berries (or cut in half if desired), turning quickly and coating each berry with glaze.

     4. Turn into baked shell and chill in refrigerator. When ready to serve, top with whipped cream.

Never-Fail Pie Crust
3 cups flour
1 1/4 cups shortening
1 teaspoon salt
5 tablespoons water
1 tablespoon vinegar
1 egg, beaten

     1. Mix flour, shortening, and salt together until crumbly.

     2. Beat together water, vinegar, and egg, and add to above mixture. Make into a ball and store in the refrigerator for awhile or make into shells and freeze. Makes 3 crusts.

Ruth Lane, Damariscotta

Dead Reckoning

My grandfather on my father's side was a great captain. But as far as educational wise, it was all dead reckoning. He could run a period of time with no watch and know when he was going to make a buoy. I tried to learn the secrets. My big thing was that someday I wanted to be a captain of a boat, going up and down the coast, and if you did, you had to know the little secrets of everything.

Avery Kelley, Beals (1990)

Strawberry-Rhubarb Pie

2 cups rhubarb, diced
1$\frac{1}{2}$ cups fresh strawberries, sliced
1 cup sugar
2 tablespoons flour
$\frac{1}{2}$ teaspoon salt
2 tablespoons butter
pastry for two-crust pie

1. Preheat oven to 400°.
2. Combine rhubarb and strawberries and put in a 9-inch pastry-lined pie plate.
3. Mix together the sugar, flour, and salt, and spread over the filling. Dot with butter.
4. Cut slits in the top crust (to allow steam to escape while pie bakes) and adjust on the pie. Bake in a hot oven for about 40 minutes, or until juice bubbles through slits and crust is browned.

Mary Blackmore, Stonington

Kathy's Strawberry Parfait Pie

1 package strawberry Jell-O
1$\frac{1}{4}$ cups boiling water
1 pint ice cream
1$\frac{1}{2}$ cups fresh strawberries, sliced, or 1 box (12-ounce) frozen strawberries, thawed and drained
baked pie shell or graham cracker crust

1. Dissolve gelatin in boiling water in a 2-quart container.
2. Add ice cream, by spoonfuls, stirring until melted. Chill until set, about 20 minutes.
3. Fold in strawberries. Pour into pie shell and chill 20 or 30 minutes, or until firm.

Kathy Kane, Surry

From *Deep Waters* magazine

Fishermen have a built-in compass—the direction of the wind.

Raspberry Pie

1 quart fresh raspberries
1½ cups sugar
¼ teaspoon salt
3 tablespoons flour
2 tablespoons butter
pastry for two-crust pie

1. Preheat oven to 425°.
2. Pick over and wash the berries and then drain well.
3. Fill a 9-inch pastry-lined pie plate with the berries. Combine the sugar, salt, and flour and spread over the berries. Dot with the butter.
4. Adjust the top crust on the pie after cutting slits to allow for escape of steam while pie bakes. Bake in a hot oven for 40 minutes or until juice bubbles through slits and crust is browned.

Mary Blackmore, Stonington

Maine Raspberry-Blueberry Tart

Crust
2½ cups all-purpose flour
½ teaspoon salt
2 teaspoons baking powder
1 stick softened butter
1 cup sugar
2 eggs
½ teaspoon vanilla
1 teaspoon milk

To make crust:
1. Sift together flour, salt, and baking powder. Set aside.
2. In another bowl, cream butter and slowly add sugar. Add eggs, one at a time, scraping sides of bowl after adding each egg. Add vanilla.
3. Slowly add dry ingredients and milk alternately, a little at a time, until all are added.
4. Chill crust for 1 hour. Preheat oven to 400°. Roll out on a lightly floured board and place gently in greased 12-inch

Spruce Head, 1989

tart pan. Pat into place about $^1/_4$-inch thick. Bake in the middle of an oven for 15 minutes or until lightly browned.

Crème Pâtissière
1 cup sugar
5 egg yolks
$^2/_3$ cup flour
2 cups boiling milk
1 teaspoon butter
$1^1/_2$ teaspoons vanilla extract
1 pint blueberries
1 pint raspberries

To make crème pâtissière: (about $2^1/_2$ cups)

1. Gradually beat sugar into egg yolks and continue beating for 2 to 3 minutes until the mixture is pale yellow and forms a ribbon. Beat in sifted flour.

2. Beating the yolk mixture, gradually pour on the boiling milk in a thin stream of droplets.

3. Pour into a saucepan and set over moderately high heat. Stir with a wire whisk, reaching all over the bottom of the pan. As sauce comes to the boil it will get lumpy, but will smooth out as you beat it. When boil is reached, beat over moderately low heat for 2 to 3 minutes to cook the flour. Be careful that custard does not scorch the bottom of the pan.

4. Remove from heat, beat in butter, and add vanilla extract. Spread custard $^1/_2$-inch thick over baked crust.

5. Pick over blueberries and raspberries and arrange in alternating circles on crème pâtissière.

Eleanor Pavloff, Goose Cove Lodge, Sunset

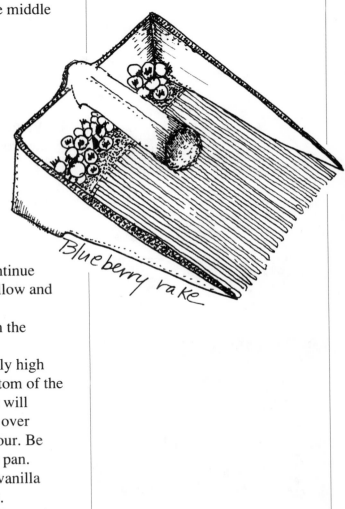
Blueberry rake

To My Wife

This day brings many memories
of the many years gone by,

When we started this trip together
just you and I.

We've had fair winds and headwinds,
and all kinds of weather, but we've never gone ashore
by pulling together.

We've sailed in the sunshine
without a ripple in sight

When life seemed all happiness
so beautiful and bright.

We've sailed through the breakers,
the crossrips and squalls,

But with some luck and some teamwork
we kept away from pitfalls.

And now with the harbor so near in sight
We should be enjoying a beautiful twilight.

But I can only look back o'er that treacherous old sea
And wish to resail it

Yes, you and me.

John D. Eastman, fisherman most of his life in Cundy's Harbor (written in 1972 for his 42nd wedding anniversary, contributed by his granddaughter, Susan Hawkes, Cundy's Harbor, who says of the poem " ... if you're married to a fisherman, happily, that is, it symbolizes your life in terms everyone understands.")

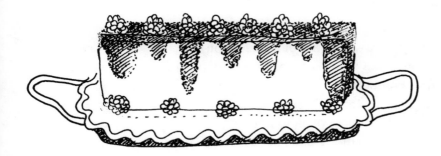

Raspberry Cake

2 cups sifted flour
$^{1}/_{2}$ teaspoon salt
3 teaspoons baking powder
$^{1}/_{3}$ cup butter
1 cup sugar
1 egg
1 teaspoon vanilla
1 cup milk
1 package frozen and drained or 1 pint fresh raspberries

     1. Preheat oven to 375°.
     2. Mix flour, salt, and baking powder.
     3. Cream butter, add sugar gradually, and mix well. Add egg and continue mixing.
     4. Stir vanilla into milk and add to creamed mixture alternately with dry ingredients.
     5. Pour into a greased 9x13-inch pan, dot with berries, and bake for 30 minutes. While cake is still warm, you may want to frost it.

Frosting (optional)
$1^{1}/_{2}$ cups confectioners sugar
1 teaspoon butter, melted
3 tablespoons cream (or enough to blend)

Paula Colwell, Deer Isle

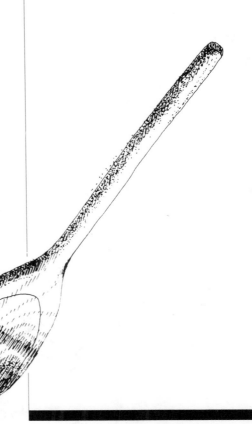

Cranberry Crunch

1 cup rolled oats (either quick or regular)
1 cup brown sugar
$^1/_2$ cup flour
1 stick margarine
cinnamon to taste (about $^1/_2$ teaspoon)
8-ounce can jellied cranberry sauce, or make your own from fresh cranberries

     1. Preheat oven to 350°.
     2. Combine oats, brown sugar, flour, margarine, and cinnamon. Spread in an 8x8-inch greased pan, reserving $^1/_2$ cup crumbs for top.
     3. Spread cranberry sauce evenly over the crumb mixture in the pan. Sprinkle with reserved crumbs. Bake for 30 to 35 minutes.

Paula Colwell, Deer Isle

Butter and Cream Baked Apples

4 large apples (Wolf River, Granny Smith, etc.)
1 cup sugar
4 tablespoons butter
1 tablespoon cornstarch
1 tablespoon cold water
$^1/_2$ cup whipping cream

     1. Preheat oven to 450°.
     2. Core, but don't peel, apples and place them in a $1^1/_2$-quart glass baking dish. Sprinkle with sugar, dot with butter, and bake for 20 to 30 minutes. Stir, baste, and turn apples twice until they are fork tender. Remove from pan.
     3. Combine cornstarch and water, add to cream, and stir into pan juices. Return apples to pan and continue to bake for another 8 to 10 minutes until sauce thickens.

Paula Colwell, Deer Isle

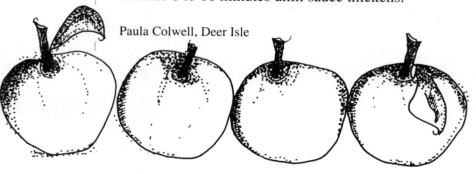

Mammy's Grapenut Pudding

3 or 4 large eggs
1 cup grapenuts
1¼ cups sugar
5 cups milk
2 tablespoons butter
2 teaspoons vanilla

    1. Preheat oven to 350°.
    2. Beat all ingredients together.
    3. Put in buttered baking dish and bake for about 45 minutes.

Roberta Joyce, Swan's Island

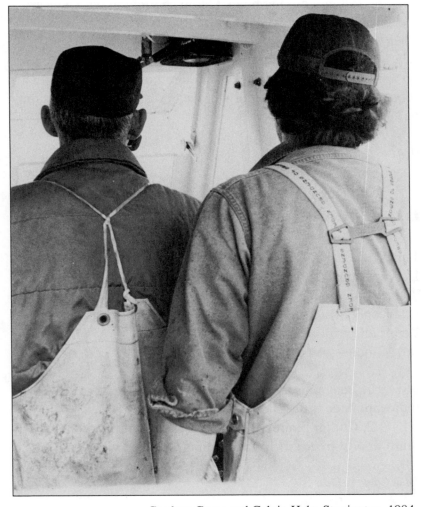

Gardner Gross and Calvin Hale, Stonington, 1984

Mottos for a Lobsterman
The first rule of lobstering is honesty, because you're on your honor when you're out there. Nothing's 100 percent in this world but the most successful fisherman is apt to be the most honest.

My grandfather told me, "It's better to come back a little bit early and live to fish another day than to stay out and try to beat the elements and not fish another day."

The only way you can tell if a man's been successful as a fisherman is when his life is over. If you're in the fishing business, and you save enough money in the good years to carry over your bad years, you're going to be successful.

You have to have a good memory to be a good fisherman. I fished in an area probably 30 miles long and 15 miles wide and on a clear day, you take me out there and if I can see, I can tell you within a few feet what's under you. The landscape out there isn't flat like the top of the ocean—it's hilly like it is in here.

A true fisherman knows that everything in the ocean has a place out there and nothing wants to be done away with. You should try to keep things in balance.

Richard Black, Bass Harbor (1990)

Harriet's Blueberry Dumplings

4 cups fresh berries
1 1/2 cups sugar

Dumplings
1 1/2 cups flour
2 teaspoons baking powder
1 teaspoon salt
3 tablespoons shortening
3/4 cup milk

    1. Cook berries and sugar with enough water to cover in a saucepan. Bring to a boil.
    2. To prepare dumplings, combine flour, baking powder, and salt in a mixing bowl. Cut in shortening with a pastry blender (or two knives) until the texture is the size of peas. Then add milk and mix.
    3. Drop dumplings into boiling berry mixture and cook 10 minutes, uncovered, and 10 minutes, covered. Serve with a scoop of vanilla ice cream or whipped cream. Blackberries may be substituted for blueberries.

Harriet Heanssler, Deer Isle

Homemade Ice Cream

4 eggs
1 1/3 cups sugar
1/2 teaspoon salt
1 tablespoon vanilla
2 cups all-purpose cream
two 12-ounce cans evaporated milk

    1. Beat eggs and then add sugar, salt, vanilla, cream, and evaporated milk. Blend all ingredients well.
    2. Chill mixture completely before putting into the churn. It will freeze in 15 to 20 minutes if cold when starting.

Paula Colwell, Deer Isle

Good-bye, Lobster

We've gazed with resignation on the passing of the auk,
Nor care a continental for the legendary rok;
And the dodo and the bison and the ornith-o-rhyn-chus
May go and yet their passing brings no shade of woe to us.
We entertain no sorrow that the megatherium
Forever and forever is departed, dead and dumb:
But a woe that hovers o'er us brings a keen and bitter pain
As we weep to see the lobster vanish off the coast of Maine.

Oh, dear crustacean dainty of the dodge-holes of the sea,
I tune my lute in minor in a threnody for thee.
You've been the nation's martyr and 'twas wrong to treat you so,
And you may not think we love you; yet we hate to see you go.
We've given you the blazes and hot-potted you, and yet
We've loved you better martyred than when living, now you bet.
You have no ears to listen, so, alas, we can't explain
The sorrow that you bring us as you leave the coast of Maine.

Do you fail to mark our feeling as we bitterly deplore
The passing of the hero of the dinner at the shore?
Ah, what's the use of living if you also can't survive
Until you die to furnish us the joy of one "broiled live"?
And what can e'er supplant you as a cold dish on the side?
Or what assuage our longings when to salads you're denied?
Or what can furnish thunder to the legislative brain
When ruthless Fate has swept you from the rocky coast of Maine?

I see, and sigh in seeing, in some distant, future age
Your varnished shell reposing under glass upon a stage,
The while some pundit lectures on the curios of the past,
And dainty ladies shudder as they gaze on you aghast.
And all the folks that listen will wonder vaguely at
The fact that once lived heathen who could eat a Thing like that.
Ah, that's the fate you're facing — but laments are all in vain—
Tell the dodo that you saw us when you lived down here in Maine.

Holman F. Day, taken from *Up in Maine* (Fourth Edition), 1901

Are we running out of lobsters?
Probably not. Although the number of traps continues to increase, lobster landings in Maine have remained remarkably stable over the last 20 years at about 20 million pounds.

Mother's Ice Cream

$^1/_2$ teaspoon gelatin
$^1/_2$ cup cold milk
$1^1/_2$ cups hot milk
1 cup sugar
1 cup cream
3 tablespoons cocoa (or any flavoring desired)

     1. Soak gelatin in cold milk until it softens. Stir in hot milk, add sugar, and cook over low heat for about 15 minutes, until slightly thickened.
     2. Remove from heat and set aside to cool. Add cream and flavoring. Put into an ice cream maker and freeze.

Lucy Kelley, Beals (handed down to Avery Kelley, Beals)

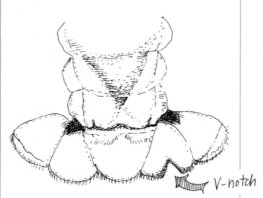

V-notch

Why are there more lobsters to catch each year?
To make sure there are always enough lobsters to catch, lobstermen follow laws and regulations to help conserve the lobster population. There is a law in Maine which states lobsters have to be a certain size to be kept. Lobstermen measure lobsters with a "gauge" to determine if they are too small or too large to keep. The theory is that small lobsters should be left in the ocean until they are large enough to reproduce at least once before they are caught. Also, large lobsters can carry many more eggs than smaller mature lobsters, so returning large lobsters to the ocean helps insure more lobsters for the future.

In addition, when a fisherman traps a lobster with eggs, he often puts a V-notch in its tail flipper and throws it back into the ocean. This mark lasts through several molts and protects the lobster because it is illegal to keep a lobster that is V-notched. It is also illegal to land a lobster with eggs. Both of these regulations help conserve lobsters.

Stonington, 1983